What the Bible Says About . . . BEING A MAN

A companion book to,
On the Other Side Of the Garden,
for women, by Virginia Fugate

by
J. Richard Fugate

Published by
Foundation for Biblical Research

All Scripture quotations are taken from the
King James Version

What the Bible Says About . . .
Being a Man

Copyright 2002 by
Foundation for Biblical Research
Citrus Heights, Ca 95610

website: www.rfugate.org
e-mail: cbg@rfugate.org

Printed in the United States of America
ISBN   1-889700-29-0

DEDICATION

to the glory of God

The author takes no personal credit for the information contained in this book. May God alone be glorified through this presentation of His Word.

Not unto us, O LORD, not unto us, but unto thy name give glory, for thy mercy, and for thy truth's sake. Psalm 115:1

The author exercises the option to utilize capitalization on personal pronouns for any member of the Godhead and words referring to the Bible or attributes of God.

ACKNOWLEDGEMENTS

EDITING by:
BILL THOMAS
And numerous other men who read and critiqued various chapters

COVER DESIGN by:
DAVID AND RACHEL VELASQUEZ (based on the painting by Edmund Blair Leighton, The Accolade, by permission of the Art Renewal Center, Port Reading, NJ)

TYPESETTING by:
DAVID AND RACHEL VELASQUEZ with Adobe Pagemaker 7.0

Other books in this series are:

What the Bible Says About . . . Child Training
ISBN 1-889700-13-4
What the Bible Says About . . . Suffering
ISBN 1-889700-35-5

PREFACE

What the Bible Says About . . . is a series designed to present the systematic development of the Bible as it speaks on specific subjects. All study is performed under the principle of 2 Timothy 2:15 *Study to show thyself approved unto God, a workman that needeth not to be ashamed, rightly dividing the word of truth.* Selected passages have been studied in depth within their contexts from the original languages of Scripture. Word studies have been performed on each word that is translated in the semantic domain of manhood. Much of the research used in the writing of this book was performed by the Foundation for Biblical Research. F.B.R. is a nonprofit (not tax exempt) organization dedicated to the discovery of the specific meaning of Scripture and the fully substantiated presentation of that meaning. The reason the author accepts the Bible as the best source of information for man is explained in Appendix A. Every reader should study the explanation of that premise before beginning this book.

The opinions, illustrations, and applications given in this book represent years of practical experience in, and observation of, men and marriages as well as the result of hundreds of personal hours in Biblical, historical, and philosophical study. The author accepts full responsibility for these opinions, illustrations, and applications. To God alone be the glory for the Biblical information revealed herein.

Foundation for Biblical Research

Recommendation: Read this book twice; the first time straight through for an overview; the second time chapter by chapter, studying each one carefully.

TABLE OF CONTENTS

SECTION THREE:

THE FUNCTIONS OF A BIBLICAL MAN – WHO SHOULD I BE?

An Explanation of Man's Biblical Role

SECTION FOUR:

THE ULTIMATE ROLE OF BIBLICAL MANHOOD – LEADERSHIP

Lead, Follow, or Get Out of the Way

APPENDICES:

WHY SHOULD I READ THIS BOOK?

The following are some of the problems many men face in today's world. Studying this book can help you overcome them on your way to…Being A Man:

Signs that a man relates to his wife as being the leader of the family.

• When he looks to her to make all of the plans for the family.
• When he tells the children to "ask your mom" for all directions.
• When he depends on his wife to decide when to leave an event.
• When he can never win in a discussion with his wife.
• When he is too intimidated to direct his wife and family.
• When he would be too afraid to show his wife a list like this.

Signs that a wife behaves as if she were in charge of the family.

• When she thinks her financial contribution makes her a full partner in the marriage.
• When she always commands him what to do.
• When she corrects him whenever he is not perfectly accurate in what he says in public.
• When she scolds him like a son if front of the children.
• When she takes over tasks he has started because she thinks he is too slow or that she has a better way.
• When he dreads coming home late, even with a valid reason, because of the third degree he will have to face.
• When she hinders him from using proper discipline on their delinquent children.

If you failed this little quiz, you need this book!

1 Samuel 4:9b *quit yourselves like men, and fight.*

1 Corinthians 16:13b *quit you like men, be strong.*

FORWARD

The above verses literally command men to, "behave themselves like grown men." Throughout history God has challenged men to be strong and manly. Following God's lead, *Being a Man*, has been written to challenge all Christian men of the 21st Century to become real men in the full, Biblical sense – men who possess masculine, mature, moral character.

Most readers are painfully aware that the modern American male falls short of manhood as God intended it to be. Today's men (including many Christians) are the products of worldly philosophies, promoted and continuously defiled by Satan. Because of a general lack of training, many men have become emasculated – insecure, passive, and fearful of displaying any masculine traits and taking their places as leaders of their families. Others have overcompensated by acting macho – boastful, forceful, and domineering (especially over women). However, no man needs to remain in either of these deplorable states. Learning about and living out Biblical manhood can transform any man's life for the better.

Since the 1950's, men in our country have become increasingly weakened in their masculinity. Most were never encouraged to "quit you like men" or to "be strong" during their childhood. That deficiency has resulted in a chronic lack of male maturity that is now reaching epidemic proportions. Several generations of boys have grown up without a father or any other masculine role model. Many of those boys, unlike boys in earlier generations, did not participate in character-building experiences during their youth. Even though experience is a poor substitute for a loving father, it did partially train a few young men for the role of manhood in the past. Boys who participated in competitive, high-school athletic programs; who were raised on a farm or developed a strong work ethic by handling a 4 a.m. paper route for several years; or who eventually enlisted in military boot camp, usually gained a certain amount of male toughness.

The purpose of this book is not to humiliate any man who may presently fall within one of these two, extreme positions. If my straight-forward, direct, bottom-line style of communication startles you at times, please avoid the temptation to become defensive. This book is meant for a large and varied audience and is not personal. If it points out weaknesses or convicts you in any way, let that conviction be what encourages you to make the changes necessary for becoming the man God desires you to be.

As you read, *What the Bible Says About ... Being a Man*, you will notice that it has none of the psychologically-based teachings so popular in the 1980's and 1990's. Those teachings have influenced many men to forsake their roles as leaders. Sadly, Christian books on manhood have also generally mimicked the world's unbalanced masculinity. Instead of teaching men how to understand and overcome their emasculated, [1] effeminate, [2] or macho [3] distortions, recent books have actually encouraged men to become more like women.Such books imply that feminine emotions, thought patterns, and spiritual awareness are superior to a man's and that true masculine maturity requires men to display these feminine characteristics and subordinate their own.Some of this teaching goes so far as to promote an unbiblical "partnership" in marriage resulting in the woman becoming a co-leader, or the man even becoming his wife's helpmate.[4] It is not that a woman's needs are unimportant, but the errors in these books have supported the unnatural reversal of Biblical roles. *Being a Man* was written to help direct the reader on a path toward balanced Biblical manhood.

The philosophy that has shaped most men's minds today has been worldly – Satan inspired, rather than Biblical – God inspired. If a man does not fortify his mind with the Word of God, he will be influenced by the worldly philosophies to which he is constantly exposed. Public opinion and the entertainment media provide most American men with the ideas that become their own opinions. Few of us realize how much we are influenced by these two sources of misinformation. For one example let us consider television's top-ranking situation comedy from 1991-1998.

Whether you watch television or not, you are probably aware of the character the talented actor/ comedian, Tim Allen, portrayed on the show, *Home Improvement.* Mr. Allen depicted the emasculated majority of today's males well. He played the part of a self-centered male, bent on getting his own way, while simultaneously trying to avoid conflict with his wife, Jill. She exemplified the modern mother-figure: required to parent her husband as much as her sons.

Tim exhibited no worthwhile moral standards except for his work ethic – and even that was dubious since his 'work' was playing himself on cable television. He played the part of a man who would not stand up and take accountability for anything – with his authorities, his wife, even his kids. Tim was depicted as a bad little boy obsessed with man's play (sports and building things with his tools); who continuously got in trouble with his mommy/wife. His occasional sorties into manhood were moments of futile machoism that ended with him looking foolish and emasculated as he begged his wife for forgiveness. Normally he did not even understand what he had done that was wrong. What a great male role model! *Home Improvement* (and its creator, Walt Disney Studios) offered us an adult male who was more like a puppy being scolded after missing his paper than a real man.

I discuss this show because of the rich examples of *incorrect* male/female relationships it presents. Popular television often entertains us with caricatures out of real-life. *Home Improvement* was considered the 1990's parallel to *Father Knows Best* of the 1950's. It supposedly depicted today's model family and the current war-between-the-sexes. The show portrays even another model of distorted manhood in Tim's sidekick, Al. This pitiful male lived primarily to please his mommy (as well as everyone else in his life). Al served as a pathetic example of today's totally effeminate male – unmanly in his traits, tastes, habits; i.e. exhibiting more feminine characteristics than masculine.

Many men, lacking correct information, will unconsciously learn their roles from this show and others like it. However, it is time for all Christian men to forsake such unbiblical examples in exchange for Biblical manhood. Such men will restore women to their place of glory and honor and then exercise balanced leadership for the sake of their families. From their Biblically-based position of authority, these men will provide for their families' needs; protect them from physical, soul, and spiritual dangers; and cherish their wives in true love. Leadership, provision, protection, and love are the badges of God's mature men in every generation.

Of course there are reasons why balanced, masculine men have all but disappeared in our country over the past fifty years. This book will explore some of these reasons and briefly review historical issues related to that demise. It has been said, "Those who cannot remember the past are condemned to repeat it." [5] Future chapters that explain the American family's historical disintegration and Satan's attack on men and women were not meant to be exhaustive. These studies are intended merely to reveal historical trends throughout history from the perspective of spiritual wisdom. After seeing these trends, we will study the make-up of mankind's soul, how the Bible defines true manhood, how the reader can overcome any personal, off-balanced training he may have received, and finally, how fathers can help train their boys to become real men.

America's men are *not* in a hopeless condition. If our God can save us each from sin (2 Timothy 1:9; Titus 3:5), He can restore our souls (2 Corinthians 4:16), renew our minds (Romans 12:2), and supernaturally empower our bodies (Isaiah 40: 29 – 31). Prayerfully, you are ready to dive into this study and learn how to live Biblical manhood. God's plan needs "a few good men" – maybe now, more than ever before. Are you willing to "be like a man and be strong"? Do you desire to serve God? Then make it your goal today ...

Phillipians 2:15 *That ye may be blameless and harmless, the sons of God, without rebuke, in the midst of a crooked and perverse nation, among whom ye shine as lights in the world.*

Notes

1. *The Compact Edition of the Oxford English Dictionary (1989), Fourth Edition, 2000, s.v.* "emasculate." to castrate; to drain of virility; to deprive of strength and vigor.

2. *Ibid.* s.v. "effeminate" to make into a woman; to represent as a woman; to make womanish or unmanly; to grow weak. (Author's comment: to emasculate a male is to make him less than a man, like an eunuch; while to effeminate a male is to make him more like a female.

3. *Roget's II The New Thesaurus , 3rd Edition (1995),* s.v. "macho" adjective; male, manly, manlike, masculine, virile; noun, machismo; one who acts macho.

4. *Journal of Marriage and the Family*, February 22,1998, *Arizona Republic* states that the newest advice from psychologists is for "men just to do what your wife says. Go ahead, give in to her." This theory is to replace *active listening* theories says Dr. John Gottman, University of Washington.

5. George Santayana (1863-1952), Philosopher
www.iupui.edu/~santedit/

SECTION ONE

WHERE ARE WE AND HOW DID WE GET HERE?

Historical, Social, Philosophical, and Spiritual Reasons

Ecclesiastes.1: 9b,10 *and there is no new thing under the sun. Is there any thing whereof it may be said, See, this is new? it hath been already of old time, which was before us.*

CHAPTER ONE

HOW HISTORICAL EVENTS HAVE AFFECTED THE AMERICAN MALE

Throughout the centuries, nations have risen to greatness based on the personal good character and righteous principles of their people. Those same nations have later fallen when their men gave up living by those principles and character. America is no different; its decline is now in process. Like a frog slowly cooking in increasingly hotter water, most of us do not recognize subtle changes in our society as they occur. However, looking backward it is easy to see those changes. Surely a time traveler from the early 1800's would experience culture shock if exposed to today's people, or the people of any of the past few generations. Indeed, I have observed a multitude of changes over the six decades of my brief life. The point is this: there are great differences in the way current generations think, act, and feel compared to those people who originally settled this country. Things truly are very different today, for instance, it was only men who originally settled America. All of the 105 settlers at Jamestown in 1607 were men. These settlers established and maintained government, business, and Church. From 1607 to approximately 1820, men in America were leaders, providers, and protectors of their families.[1]

By contrast, most men today avoid the role of leadership in their homes as well as in Church, business, and government. They shun leadership partly because they fear taking accountability for the decisions they would then have to make. Joshua's declaration, *but as for me and my house, we will serve the LORD* (Joshua 24:15), would have been politically incorrect today. Few husbands would dare to make such a decision without first seeking their wife's approval, or even her leadership. Our country desperately needs a return of real men like Joshua who will stand up for Biblical truth against "politically correct" false doctrines.

There were very few major changes in society for the first 200 years of America's agrarian (living off the land) history. Prior to about 1840, families were self-sufficient – growing or making almost everything they consumed. The average family had seven children who were an integral part of the family economy and who were schooled at home. Then, the Industrial Revolution totally changed American life from 1840 to 1940 A.D. The family unit became restructured during this period. Fathers left the homestead to work in the city and the men/father influence in society began to decrease. [2] Most home functions (growing food, making clothes, building furniture, training the children) had to be abandoned. It was during this time that women/mothers, instead of men/fathers, gradually became the moral leaders of home, family, school, Church, and social reform.

Women soon began to fill the vacuum left in each of these areas. While men became heavily involved in the Industrial Revolution, women were being influenced by the Victorian era. Millions of copies of romantic novels from Europe flooded America, glorifying the new role of the woman. Women quickly came to think of themselves as the moral leaders of society – the champions for justice and crusaders of the downtrodden and disadvantaged. Men would be allowed to rule commerce; women would rule everything else. You probably remember the joke, "Yes, I am the boss of my house. I let my wife make all of the little decisions: buying of cars, making investments, and the planning the kid's college; I make all the big decisions like world peace, space travel, and taking out the garbage."

In the male-deserted classrooms and Sunday schools of the 1850's, women began to fill the vacancies for teachers. Men had previously held almost all of these positions. By 1890, women comprised 67 percent of all the public school teachers and were the majority of children's teachers in Sunday school as well. From their new positions of influence in the Church and society, women began to exercise their intense social consciousness – outside of the home. They gradually became involved in the temperance movement that had been started in 1826 by a group of pastors. By 1874, they had their own arm of the movement, the Women's Christian Temperance Union. Eventually, the 18th amendment (Prohibition) was ratified in 1920. A movement that had started to combat drunkenness and promote moderation had been changed into a forceful demand for total abstinence. [3,4]

Women also took over the abolitionist movement, which in about 1833 was originally named, The American Anti-Slavery Society. In 1849 the name was changed to the Women's Abolitionist Movement. When the 15th Amendment was ratified in 1870, granting black men the right to vote, the need for this cause ended. Women naturally crusaded for their own cause also – their right to vote. Suffrage began about 1849, joined with the temperance movement in 1890, and reached its objective upon the ratification of the 19th amendment in 1920. The following chart presents a chronology of women's moral/ social causes in America during this period:

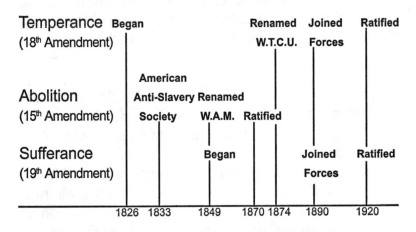

Figure 1.1 Women's Movements of the 1800's

America's women had definitely made their presence and power known by 1920. Winning the right to vote meant that women could legally negate men's vote on any political issue. This also meant that women had moved from having no power politically to having equal power with men. Politicians immediately began to appeal to the social consciousness of the woman's vote. Men in America have not recovered political leadership since that time. The women's vote has been a major contributor in electing every social-issues politician since the 1920's, especially by their landslide votes for Bill Clinton in 1992 and 1996. [5]

The social issues women promote (including voting for anyone who *says* he/she supports them) are health, education, and welfare. They champion laws to protect children (orphanages and work prohibitions); to relieve poverty (food and clothing for the destitute); to prevent harsh justice (prison reform and abolishing capitol punishment); to provide cradle-to-the-grave education; and, to prevent private gun ownership and national preparations for war. While some of these are *bona fide* issues, their solutions are more the responsibility of the Church and personal accountability than that of government. But after the women won the vote, their proper, nurturing instincts were unleashed from the home and overtook government. From their new position of power they have been attempting to eliminate mankind's suffering through legislation for the past eighty years.

Were women's issues improved by their gaining political power? Do you think America is better off today, particularly in the areas of women's greatest influence – health, education, and welfare? Each of these areas have been funded to the point of nearly bankrupting the nation. However, our public education now produces the lowest results in our nation's history, our social security/retirement system is totally insecure, and our welfare system is a windfall for swindlers. Obviously, the women's right to vote has not solved the injustices of mankind.

By 1920, men had effectively lost (actually just gave up) their leadership in the home, Church, and social programs – and they didn't seem to care. It meant that women were taking on all of the responsibilities in those areas. Fathers became figureheads – leaders without power; while " the hand that rocks the cradle" became the real power in the home and in the country. Men did continue to function in their roles as providers and protectors of their families in the early 20th century. Considering their Victorian-like wives to be morally and spiritually superior to themselves, men abdicated most leadership roles to them. Did women gain personally in either consideration or respect from their 200-year crusade? Note the following story from the early 1800's I heard about thirty years ago:

> *It has been said that an Eastern newspaperman went "down South" prior to the Civil War to interview the southern ladies. He had heard they were more feminine, desirable, and submissive to their husbands than were their counterparts back East, and he desired to know why. After his interviews, he wrote an article stating that, "The difference with southern women is . . . southern men." His article continued to describe how southern gentlemen treated their wives and daughters with total respect and honor. In other words, the wives were cherished and the women's response was to live up to their reputation of being noble ladies.*

The Generations of the 1900's

Between 1914 and 1945, three catastrophic events magnified the impact of the Industrial Revolution on mankind. World War I, the Great Depression, and World War II decimated manhood in America and tore at the fabric of the family. The cumulative effect of these events affected child training, politics, and family life to this very day. A century of such tumultuous changes as the 20th Century experienced, requires further analysis.

The changes in society came so rapidly in the 1900's that each generation was identified by its own specific characteristics. This book will use the word "generation" to stand for a group of people born within a specific period and having basically similar characteristics.[6] (Statisticians and social scientists generally agree on the time brackets and classifications given herein.) [7]

Naturally, not every individual born within one of the following time periods fits that generation's profile, while others born a little before or after might fit perfectly. And, of course, some individuals within any generation march to their own drumbeat. The following chart attempts to depict a general chronology of the generations of the past 100 years. None of these dates or profiles are written in stone, they are merely human classifications.

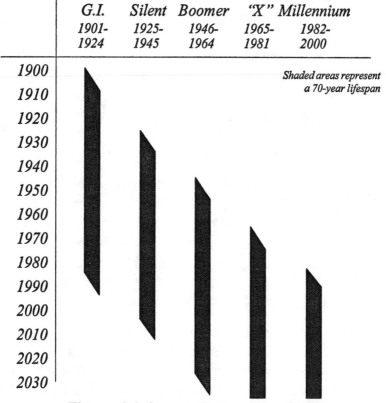

Figure 1.2 Generations of the 1900's

Now that we have seen the recent generations laid out against a historical backdrop, let us see what is behind those unusual labels.

• **The GI** (Government Issue) **Generation**: those born roughly between 1901 and 1924. This name may not be a widely held identification, but it is descriptive. This generation supplied soldiers(GI's) for both World War I and World War II. They fought and overcame difficult obstacles — war, plague, and economic depression. The worldwide influenza epidemic of 1918 and 1919 killed 20 million people – 500,000 in America alone (many more than the 116,500 GI's who died in the same 19 months "over there.") The men of this generation who survived became stronger in character and many taught their boys basic traits of manhood. (From my studies, I believe these children became the cream of the next generation, if not of the entire century.)

• **The Silent Generation**: those born from 1925 to 1945. This generation as well survived the Great Depression and World War II. They had experienced deprivation, fear, insecurity, and suffering. Generally speaking this generation didn't make waves — they were strong but silent. They were independent, self-sufficient, and private.

• **The Boomer Generation**: those born from 1946 to 1964. This generation is named for its 76 million babies (an increase of 17 million above normal). They comprised 31 percent of their adult population and since their birth they have been like a pig going through a boa constrictor. Their sheer numbers have dominated entertainment, culture, politics, and product purchases since at least the 1960's. Warning: The demographic bulge of baby boomers will overwhelm the USA's already over-burdened social security system by 2020. A word to the wise, plan your own retirement.

• **The "X" Generation**: those born from 1965 to 1981(also called The Busters and The 13th Generation). This generation is the unknown quantity as it has yet to make any major impact on society. They seem to be seeking for truth in life, but have few absolutes with which to compare information.

• **The Millennial Generation**: those born from 1982 to 2000 (yet to be determined The Next, The "Y," or The "Z" Generation). Those born from 2001 to 2020 (if the world as we know it continues that long).

The next chapter will show exactly how these multiple generations affected the American family and especially the American male.

Notes:

1. *Missing From Action*, by Weldon Hardenbrook, 2nd edition, January 1996, Conciliar Press. In chapter four of this book, the author compiles the research of three other writers who have written about early American history (prior to 1820): *Womanhood in America*, by Mary P. Ryan; *Be A Man*, by Peter N. Sterns; and *Virginians at Home*, by Edmund S. Morgan.

2.*Cottage to Work Station*, by Allan C. Carlson. This scholarly text well covers the history of how and why our country moved from the farm to an industrialized society and at what cost to family members, March 1993, Ignatius.

3. An interesting side note concerning the effectiveness of the mostly-women lead fight for prohibition:

> a) The Temperance Movement did destroy and otherwise force a large percentage of local brewers and pubs temporarily out of business. These vigilantes even destroyed the private property of those who would not submit to their demands for morality. Crusades always trample the rights of others in their self-righteous zeal.
> b) However, Prohibition put a lot of petty thugs into business and allowed crime to organize from 1920 to 1933. The demand for alcohol did not decrease just because it was outlawed. Politicians and many of the police in most major cities became corrupt protecting the bootleggers and speakeasies.
> c) After 14 years of women's victory in legislating morality, Prohibition was repealed. The 100-year battle for temperance had been lost with no gain, but with much cost. Besides the political corruption, much of which we have inherited today, the Temperance Movement's short-lived success may well have spawned The Mafia. Certainly thousands of families had to suffer without the wives' and mothers' influence and support during the time they were out pursuing their crusade.

4. Hardenbrook, *Missing From Action*, (Ibid.),Chapter 6

5. Internet research on the women's vote (multiple sources).

6.*Oxford English Dictionary*, s.v. "generation;" 1. the action of begetting or procreating; generation of plants or animals; offspring, progeny, descendants, or posterity. 2. General; entire body of individuals living about the same time period, or the time covered by their births; from the birth of parents to the birth of their children, approximately three generations per 100 years (now 18-20 years each); a family, breed, class, or race of people."

7. *Generations: The History of America's Future,1584 – 2069*, by William Strauss and Neil Howe, Morrow & Co.,1991.

Hosea 8:7 *For they have sown the wind, and they shall reap the whirlwind:*

Job 4: 8 *Even as I have seen, they that plow iniquity, and sow wickedness, reap the same.*

CHAPTER TWO

HISTORY'S EFFECT ON THE AMERICAN FAMILY

The first three generations of the 20th Century profoundly impacted the American family and its men in particular. By the year 1935, everyone from ten years old and older (the G.I. and Silent Generations) had experienced World War I and the Great Depression. Almost all of the survivors were tough and frugal (they would straighten a bent nail for reuse). But, these catastrophes also made them insecure – uncertain about the future. Wanting to ensure that their children would never experience war or live through the same deprivation they had suffered, these survivors supported almost any polititian's promise to eliminate the risks and dangers from life. They allowed the establishment of a world government (League of Nations/United Nations) and the implementation of President Roosevelt's master plan to socialize America. The FICA, TVA, REA, FTC, and FAA, were only a few of many new programs of FDR's New Deal ostensibly created for our well-being. (These government programs, and hundreds added since, have weakened the character of American men with the false promise of protection and provision. They have also robbed each man of a large portion of his income and incentive to save.) To many, government became expected to take the place of God's provision for mankind. By the time World War II ended in 1945, most Americans were shell-shocked and ready to accept any politician, program, or minister that eased their fears about the future.

The men and women of the G.I. and Silent Generations were moral, God-fearing, industrious, financially frugal, self-reliant, and authoritarian in child training. When it came to religion, most adults claimed to be Christians (by which many only meant that they observed the Ten Commandments outwardly). However, there was little real zeal in presenting Jesus Christ as a personal Savior.

This generation was comprised of very private people. They threw themselves into hard work and protected their children from experiencing any hardships. This supposed 'protection' even included being secretive about family finances or problems. Generally, they wanted to trust the government and experts (like Dr. Benjamin Spock). As a result, they did not stand up against the evils in society. They were silent about our government's increasing move toward socialism; they remained silent about our country's involvement and no-win policy in Korea and Vietnam. They quietly allowed the public schools to move away from educational basics, the Church to move away from teaching the Bible, and the media to move away from any common decency.

Along came the boom years of the 1950's and jobs were abundant. Some men held two jobs for years and/or attended night school, all to provide material abundance for their families. During wartime people had money to buy things, but everything had been in short supply; during the depression there had been lots of things for sale, but no money to buy them; now there was plenty of money and a boundless supply of old and new products. The 1950's was the most financially prosperous decade of this century for the average working family. But the children suffered horribly from the resulting materialism.

The 1950's began the decades of the totally missing fathers. Many Dads found little time for child training, camping, sporting events, school activities, Church, or anything else with their children. Some fathers attempted to assuage their guilt by buying whatever their children wanted. Showering their children with prosperity, these dads seemed unaware of the role that hardship and suffering had played in forging their own characters. Instead, they continued to shield their children from the realities of life, while treating them permissively. It should be of no surprise that the anti-materialistic, immature, rebellious gypsies of the 1960's and 1970's resulted from this upbringing. Few young people from the 'boom' generation became mature adults without spending many years later going through the school of hard knocks to make up for their deficiency in child training.

You might ask,"What difference does this make to me? I am around thirty-years-old and living in the 21st Century." However, you are the son, or at least the grandson, of parents who did live through this period. The training your father and grandfather received influenced how they trained you. Their standards may not have been bad, but one seldom sees standards become higher (better, more moral, more godly) from one generation to the next. The present generation is always affected by whom our forefathers were, both personally and generally.

Children raised in the 1940's and 1950's (The Boomer Generation) became the young adults of the 1960's and

1970's. These were the children abandoned by their fathers and in many cases even by working mothers. They grew up hating materialism, and were starved for family and a sense of belonging. They detested their parents' weak leadership and therefore rejected all authorities. One popular saying was, "Don't trust anyone over thirty." The Peace Corps and many cults (which often claimed absolute authority and insisted upon communal ownership of personal possessions) flourished during these years. Once pampered children became idealistic, social liberals. They accepted few Biblical standards for right and wrong and participated in immoral sexual and drug revolutions without so much as a pained conscience. This generation was so self-centered they actually came to be known as the "Me" generation. (I personally believe that the Boomer Generation is the first of the four cursed generations warned about in Exodus 20:5 and expounded on in Proverbs 30:11-14, *There is a generation that curseth their father, and doth not bless their mother.*)

The 1960's also brought the demoralizing, "undeclared war" in Vietnam (1961 to 1972) following America's contrived defeat in the "undeclared war" in Korea (1950 to 1953). In both of these "non-wars," our government chose to send American troops to die, but not to allow our generals to win. America became a paper tiger in actuality while operating under the non-committed leadership of the time. It is no wonder that the flower children and draft-dodgers could not make any sense out of our government's policies. And, if the "non-wars" were not enough, there was the fiasco at the Bay of Pigs, the building of the Berlin wall, and the assassination of President Kennedy (1963) to add to their disillusionment. Then The Watts Riots shot a hole in their philosophy that, "everybody should love everybody." With their altruistic ideals wounded, if not dead, all the Boomers had left to live for was drugs, sex, and their music.

The latchkey kids of the 1970's (Generation X) became adults in the 1980's with little idea whom they were or what they were supposed to do. Having virtually raised themselves, their understanding of reality was shaped by their peers and the ever-present entertainment media. Convinced that the earth was running out of food, water, and air, they were depressed about their future. These children had also been brainwashed into accepting the lie of evolution. Consequently, they believed that they were not a product of creation by a loving God who had a plan for their lives. They felt hopeless about their economic future knowing that the previous generations had put them deeply in debt. Lacking self-discipline, they expected immediate results for anything they endeavored. And, of course, they expected the government to pay all of their bills as Mom and Dad had always done. Sex meant disease and drugs meant addiction to them. This may well be the second generation of the Biblical curse; *There is a generation that are pure in their own eyes, and yet is not washed from their filthiness* (Proverbs 30:12).

The current generation of new adults (the Millennial Generation, those born from about 1982 to 2000), are said to be disrespectful, self-centered, materialistic, and technologically savvy. They have had virtually no positive role models. If this is the third generation of our Biblical curse, they will be: *a generation, O how lofty are their eyes! and their eyelids are lifted up.* (i.e. proud) (Proverbs 30:13).

It is interesting that today's children (the Y Generation, born 2001 and after) will reach adulthood about the same time Social Security becomes impossible to fund. This could be the final generation. The following passage indicates that these fourth-generation children will not take care of their parents and grandparents when the government fails: *a generation, whose teeth are as swords, and their jaw teeth as knives, to devour the poor from off the earth, and the needy from among men* (Proverbs 30:14).

Yes, life in these United States is very different today than it was a few generations ago! The early settlers were strong, self-reliant people. They bartered or paid cash for everything. It was considered a sin to be in debt. They accepted God's gracious control over all things and knew there was no guarantee of life, health, or happiness. Men and women understood and accepted their individual roles in life. There was little competition between each other. Children were raised to know God, to obey their parents, and to respect all adults. Adulthood was a privilege a child earned, not a right given. Their education was superior to the public schools of the last 100 years – children could read well by age three or four and learned their first lessons from the Bible. Most began formal education about seven years old and were ready to enter colleges like Yale or Harvard at age 13 or 14, after having already mastered Greek, Hebrew, grammar, Ancient History, and math.[1] We have fallen woefully far behind those achievements today.

Sumary

This book asserts the position that objective, Biblical standards for measuring manhood (which we will later describe) do exist and that at certain periods throughout history men have met these standards. However, I also believe it can be shown the average man falls far short of them today.

- The men who settled America from 1607 to 1840 A.D. accepted the responsibilities of leadership, protection, and provision for their families. It could also be shown that they normally honored and respected their wives.

- Rather than aspire to Biblical Manhood, most men today are content to be: emasculated (having lost the characteristics of a man); effeminate (taking on the characteristics of a woman); or macho (employing crude, animal-like characteristics without consideration for the feelings or rights of others, especially women).

- Major historical events and trends over the last one hundred years partially explain why today's grandfathers, fathers, and sons have developed into such aberrations from God's revealed norm. A more detailed examination of such events would include:

  - decreasing acceptance of the Bible as the standard for life;
  - the Industrial Revolution;
  - the Civil War;
  - the Great War (WW I);
  - the Great Depression;
  - World War II;
  - compulsory education and subsequent lowering of basic academics;

- the move away from classical education to liberal arts; [2]
- America's conversion from a Republic to a Democracy;
- the expansion of social welfare programs;
- the general acceptance of the theory of evolution (making man no more than an animal without purpose or reason for life);
- the abundant prosperity of the 1950's;
- changes in the goals and methods of child training;[3]
- absentee parents, beginning with fathers and by 1960 including approximately 40% of mothers working outside the home;
- the huge increase in divorces, even among Christians.

It might seem reasonable to excuse any mistakes these people made based on the truly difficult challenges they experienced. However, the circumstances in a person's life do not determine his character. Rather, it is how a person or group of persons (like a country) deals with those circumstances that matter. People are not victims of the events in history; they chose to conquer life or allow it to defeat them. Although many of the individuals passed some or even all of the tests, this book sets forth the position that *our nation did not pass*. Individual Christian men must now make an about face if they are to restore the nation.

2 Chronicles 7:14 *If my people, which are called by my name, shall humble themselves, and pray, and seek my face, and turn from their wicked ways; then will I hear from heaven, and will forgive their sin, and will heal their land.*

Are you ready? Have we reaped the whirlwind long enough? If men will not lead their families (wives and children), the Church, politics, business, and education – this nation will continue to become weaker and subject to external attacks, as even recent history testifys. I pray that your resolve will soon match William Merrill's great hymn;

> *Rise up, o men of God!*
> *Have done with lesser things*
> *Give heart and soul and mind and strength*
> *To serve the King of Kings.*

Notes:

1. *Will Early Education Ruin Your Child?* by J. Richard Fugate; Pensacola Christian College, P.O. Box 18000, Pensacola, FL 32523-9160 (a 2nd edition of this book is to be published about mid-2002 for continued use in PCC's graduate program)

2. Examples: the learn-to-read approach changed from the 300-year, time- tested phonics method to the ineffective, look/say method; and the study of history/geography changed to social studies. *Why Johnny Still Can't Read;* Rudolph Flesch; HarperCollins, 1983

3. Due to the move away from Biblical child-training methods and purposes (even by Christians), I wrote my first book, *What the Bible Says About ... Child Training,* 1980; published now by the Foundation for Biblical Research; cbg@rfugate.org.

Proverbs 22:6 *Train up a child in the way he should go: and when he is old, he will not depart from it.*

Malachi 4:6 *And he shall turn the heart of the fathers to the children, and the heart of the children to their fathers, lest I come and smite the earth with a curse.*

CHAPTER THREE

WHEN FATHERS ABANDON THEIR SONS

Soon after the war was over in 1945, several factors converged at about the same time.

- America was beginning to experience tremendous prosperity.

- Men were gone long hours from home to obtain that prosperity.

- Women were running the homes and the schools.

- Behavioral psychology (child-centered parenting) was influencing these mothers, as per Dr. Spock.

These factors led to a lack of masculine training of little boys in America. From about 1950 on, boys have virtually been brought up in a women-dominated environment. Between World War II and the prosperity of the 50s, fathers were often absent from the home and therefore unable to influence their boys properly. Little boys were surrounded by women caregivers almost all the time. They had mothers at home, female teachers at school, and even women Sunday school teachers in most cases. (At school the janitor, the coach, and possibly the principals might still have been men, but women filled over 90 percent of the teaching positions.) Fathers were all but absent from home and, consequently, did not show their boys much about being real men. In fact, fathers were also deserting their daughters from experiencing an example of Biblical manhood and not encouraging them to pursue Biblical womanhood.

Therefore, absentee fathers were at least half of the problem of boys not being trained for masculinity (and girls not being trained for their roles). Men of this period tended to avoid an active role in their marriages and parenting. They spent themselves in the areas they could handle: making money and pursuing self-interests – personal play, school, or entertainment. They did not spend much time character training their sons in such necessary qualities as: loyalty, honesty, trustworthiness, honor, courage, bravery, self-discipline, self-sacrifice, compassion, respect for women, etc. As a result, these boys were denied essential training in being a man. The following chart depicts their predicament:

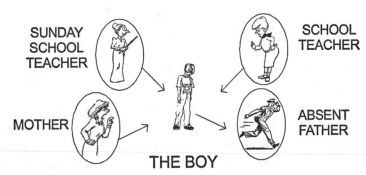

Figure 3.1 Female Influence on School-Aged Boys

So What?

Aren't mothers and other women able to train boys? In some ways, yes. But boys and girls are not the same and must be trained differently. What was that ancient nursery rhyme?

> *"What are little girls made of?*
> *Sugar and spice and all that is nice,*
> *that is what little girls are made of."*

> *"What are little boys made of?*
> *Frogs and snails and puppy dog tails,*
> *that is what little boys are made of. "*

While generally girls are all nice and sweet with just a hint of spice; boys are jumpy, wiggly, and slimy. Obviously, boys have problems that need to be repaired. Even a cursory observation of a preschool play yard today will reveal that boys are still up to their old tricks. Aggression seems to motivate their every activity. They run, compete, and attempt to dominate; they push, threaten, test, challenge, and explore; they roughhouse, and tumble. They love bodily contact and insist on there being a winner in every endeavor.

It is no surprise that women naturally detest certain facets of the male's character. Male aggression, often uncleanness, risk-taking, being academically lazy, and generally uncouth are not very lady like. Mothers and female teachers alike have long tried to restrict the supposedly negative and unseemly traits of boys and thus make them a little more like the sugar and spice, genteel, and well-mannered girls. Certainly, ladies did not mean anything wrong when they tried to eliminate toy guns from the hands of boys after all those wars. (Of course, without a gun the boys just picked up a stick or a doll's leg and said, "bang.") Neither were these women being malicious when they tried to soften the corners on untrained boys. However, they knew little about how to develop boys' masculinity correctly. That is how it should be. This was the job Dad should have been doing. However, without Dad, the tendency over the past 50 years has been to hand boys over to the female caregivers to be raised more like women than men.

One serious error in treating boys and girls the same occurred in academics sometime after women ended up in charge of education. Boys somehow got the impression that they were stupid and/or slow academically - especially in reading. While it is true that boys have difficulty with social interaction, eye-brain interactions, and attentiveness; they can learn academics when properly taught. If it were not for the offsetting error that girls have an inherent lack of ability in mathematics, boys (as well as girls) would probably have grown up thinking they were totally inferior academically to girls in everything! When well-meaning female teachers additionally tried to force social skills on boys – public speaking, taking turns, being still – it was like stroking a cat's fur the wrong way. However, these errors were not nearly as damaging as the emasculation of the boys' souls. Often, little boys would be ridiculed for their boyish actions and apparent academic deficiencies (no wonder that the majority of boys learned to hate school by highschool).

Can you imagine the game, King of the Mountain, being changed from one where each boy's bravery, courage, and leadership was tested; to a girl's game where everyone holds hands and circles the mountain playing like it was a fairy castle, or marched around it seven times like it was Jericho? The boys would likely be told not to push or pull in line or even to touch the sand. The teacher might be heard to say something like, "Can't we all be nice and just get along?"

This behavioral conditioning away from masculinity has been disastrous for the past three generations of male adults graduating into society. Nobody seemed to realize that when the aggression is completely trained out (and/or shamed out) of a boy, it can produce a man who will not fight to provide for or protect his wife or family. Women had no idea that taking away a boy's competitiveness might result in his becoming a loser in the highly competitive game of life that most breadwinners must play. (A sensitivity training game was developed for children called, "The Un-game." It was popular with psychologists, Christian teachers, and mothers because there was no competition – no winners or losers; and because it dealt with mostly feminine interests. I doubt that many lads were taught by this game to act like real men.)

Boys do need to learn how to control their aggression properly, but men who have been taught that all competitiveness is wrong will not likely strive for leadership positions in business, military, or government (or even in their own homes). I have served on the Board of Directors of several corporations and churches. Although serving with good men, mostly Christians, it seemed that the ones who graduated high school after the 1960's had difficulties making decisions on tough issues, especially if they thought someone might question their reasoning or motives afterward. Leadership requires moral courage and the willingness to stand accountable for one's actions, even when wrong.

Of course, fathers still have to take total responsibility for any lack of training of their sons' masculinity. It would not have occurred without their avoidance of fatherhood. Most men in the 21st century have been raised mostly by female caregivers. In many cases fathers did not even know what to teach their sons about being a man. Indeed, most of *their* dads did not know. It will be a lot more difficult to solve the problem now than it would have been 50 years ago. *But, the problem could still be solved in one generation.* First, fathers will need to discover Biblical manhood for themselves and then teach their sons quality character traits by word and by deed. Until that happens, our country will continue accepting the consequences of our lack of proper masculine leadership.

Where Did All Our Character Go?

The quality of men's character in America has steadily declined over the past 50 years. By character, of course, I am referring to whom a person really is in their soul. Our character governs what we do, or do not do, when we believe no one will find us out. Civilized nations in history were those that were governed by a system of just laws – societies that considered the rights of others and had a moral code of ethics. Male citizens in particular were trained to conduct themselves with honesty, trustworthiness, loyalty, bravery, and courage.

Ancient Greece, the Roman Republic, Great Britain, and America were all civilized for at least some portion of their greatness. The opposite of civilization is a mob of ignorant and selfish humans, i.e. savages. Sadly, this is the direction America has been moving since the 1950's. Instead of honesty, our country has experienced a major increase in cheating – from high school students to cadets at West Point Military Academy; and even on routine employment applications. Personal bankruptcies (legalized theft) are up over 500% since 1980 and increasing annually.[1] Instead of trustworthiness, Americans have consistently failed to honor their word on marriage vows [2] and every other type of legal contract imaginable. The legal system is even being used to extort and/or steal from the innocent parties of legitimate contracts.

Other miscellaneous tears in our fabric are being revealed as the savage seeks to come out of the untrained male. Uncontrolled rage appears in public businesses, in the auto beside you, in our schools and churches, and in our homes. Births to unwed mothers accounted for 1.29 million of the 3.94 million total births in1998. (That is nearly one-third!)[3] And, our people have become more and more dependent on the government, as they are sheared by larger and larger taxes while they receive smaller and smaller doles. Civilized people provide for their own welfare; savages demand to be fed, housed, and taken care of medically by others, *or else*!

It should be clear that America at this time is closer to being savage than it is to being civilized. Look at the fact that abortions can be freely obtained by school-aged children! A combination of the matriarchal society (especially concerning school-age boys) and absent fathers (for training boys into men of character) set up the current demise of America. I should say, of course, that not every little boy in America was ruined in the past nor are they all being ruined today. I am also not implying that all that is necessary to train boys is to allow them to rough and tumble all day. Remember, we are only trying to study the *trends* in society and their effect on the masculinity of our nation's men.

I imagine most fathers can sense their own guilt in not investing more time with their sons and daughters. I know that tears overcome me every time I identify my own failures when I hear the song *The Cat's in the Cradle*,[4] by Sandy and Harry Chapin. The words of that song appear to have been penned by a man who obviously had been such a deserting father, or worse, was the deserted son.

Are you willing to commit yourself to stop abandoning your sons and to make the sacrifice necessary to train them to be men? Of course, this means that you will need to commit to learn and practice Biblical manhood yourself. You and your son *could* learn and become mature together.

Notes

1. *American Bankruptcy World*, internet report statistics on bankruptcies: from 287,570 in 1980 and rapidly increased to 1,452,000 in 2001.

2. *Barna Research Group*, Ventura, CA; www.barna.org; "August 6, 2001 Press Release" (See chart on opposite page)

3. *The Arizona Republic*, March 2000

4. You can find the words to the song at http://harrychapin.com/music/cats.shtml

Co-Habitation, Marriage and Divorce (base:7043 adults 18+, national)

	have co-habited	have never been married	have been married	% of those married who have ever been divorced	sample size
all adults	33%	27%	73%	34%	7043
born-again Christians	25	19	81	33	2901
non born-again adults	39	32	68	34	4142
Catholics	36	27	73	29	1570
Protestants	30	22	78	32	3812
Age:under 35	44	58	42	20	2426
Age:35-49	34	14	86	39	2155
Age:50+	18	6	94	36	2328
White	34	21	79	34	4839
Black	31	38	62	36	964
Hispanic	31	41	59	32	834

NOTE:
Born again Christians are just as likely to get divorced as are non-born again adults. Overall, 33% of all born again individuals who have been married have gone through a divorce, which is statistically identical to the 34% incidence among non-born again adults.

Proverbs 10:1b *a foolish son is the heaviness of his mother.*

Proverbs 17:21 *He that begetteth a fool doeth it to his sorrow: and the father of a fool hath no joy.*

CHAPTER FOUR

THE EFFECTS OF MATRIARCHY ON BOYS

When women rule a young boy's every movement, he tends to be pressed toward one of two extremes. (This is my unscientific opinion after observing thousands of young men in schools, athletics, marriages, counseling, as employees, plus Biblical examples and confirmation from men after my speeches on the subject.) The following chart depicts a boy surrounded by exclusively female influences. Under these unnatural conditions, I believe boys with naturally strong masculine egos are likely to become very macho, while boys with more passive egos tend to be squeezed toward effeminacy.

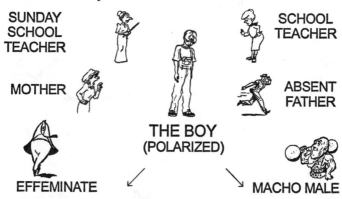

SUNDAY SCHOOL TEACHER

SCHOOL TEACHER

MOTHER

ABSENT FATHER

THE BOY (POLARIZED)

EFFEMINATE

MACHO MALE

Figure 4.1 Tendency of Polarizing Boys' Masculine Attitudes

Macho Males As Children

Macho males are at one extreme pole of masculinity. These boys tend to develop a deep anger against women throughout their years of being exposed to almost exclusively matriarchal influences. Macho males were probably the most masculine boys from the beginning (loud, rowdy, and/or clumsy). Like one young mother told me, her boy was born riding a bicycle and throwing a football. By the time every male is 10 to 13 years old, macho or not, his hormones make him feel a little macho – like a boss over all women. God is preparing these males for leading, protecting, and providing for their eventual wives and families. It is now that a father's influence is *essential* to control these aggressive feelings and to teach their sons about God's plan for their lives. They must be required to learn that respect for womanhood is a key part of true masculinity.

A strongly masculine boy's aggression can be controlled by his dad – helping him also to develop self-discipline. Excess male hormones can be redirected into strenuous work (chopping wood, painting the house, or digging mom a flower garden– some task worthy of a man-in-training). Athletic activity can also be used (physical self-improvement or *supervised* sports). Let me emphasize that all of these activities should be personally supervised by the father as much as possible. It is the corrective action taken by a father for a son's unacceptable behavior which is a key part of his training process. The other part is the father's teaching what it really takes to be a Biblical man, a Biblical husband, and a Biblical father. Your son will not learn these things by your words alone. He needs to see that your words are practiced in your everyday life. This is a great reason for dads to practice their Christianity.

Danger! If a macho-type son sees his father cower under the aggressive, noncompliant attitude of his mother and settle for peace at any cost, his soul may be further damaged. This son could develop tremendous anger against his mom (and thereby all womanhood) for humiliating his father (all men). He may even vow never to allow a woman to talk back to him. (How sad it is for the poor woman who marries any such undeveloped macho male.) His attitude toward his father will probably be one of resentment and anger at his weakness. Parents who do not train their children properly seem either to replicate their own negative characteristics and practices into them; or to produce children with opposite and equally unacceptable qualities. Do not despair if you are late in starting manhood training with your son, he is probably just waiting for you. Apologize if fitting, lay out your new plan (not more than you *will* do), and then, do it! You will be judged by your son on the basis of your follow through, especially if you have failed him in the past.

Macho Males As Adults

In adulthood these undeveloped macho males usually continue their anger against women. (When their wives try to tell them something or, *dare* to question them about anything, they can become almost violent.) Like most untrained children, these men refuse to accept accountability for their actions and of course they believe they never make a mistake. We have had examples of this kind of man on television sitcoms (extreme personalities always make the best caricatures). Archie Bunker (*All In The Family*) was designed by its author as a model of social *incorrectness*. That series' creator intended for him to be ridiculed for his politically conservative comments, but instead his unsophisticated, macho opinions were widely applauded by men throughout America. The profane Al Bundy (*Married With Children*) was an example of a wimp with macho attitude.

Sadly, millions of men identified themselves *positively* with these characters. This should alert us to the number of undeveloped macho males that exist today. These males do not just ruin their own lives, they ruin many others as well. They are insecure in their maleness, so life is a constant struggle to prove themselves. By engaging in frequent physical contests with other macho males, by dominating and using all women for their own purposes, and by dictatorially ruling their homes they attempt to justify the purpose for their existence. Their spiritual lives are usually superficial, if apparent at all. Finally, they tend to fall apart when their physical strength fails them – an excellent time to reach them for self-examination and faith in Christ. If you identify yourself as being one of these undeveloped macho males, or even partially so, please study this book for help in overcoming this severe problem. Yes, there is hope. I personally suffered with the plague of machismo for the first 45 years of my life. What is worse, my wife and family suffered with me.

I dropped out of college at 18 and got married as an already failure in life. At least I had a woman who was devoted to me and who thought she needed me. In my deep insecurity and constant depression, I dominated my household for years. Other fathers talked about changing diapers, washing clothes and dishes, helping their wives around the house. As a totally macho male, I could brag that I had never changed the diaper on any of our three children or washed anything but me. Sure, my wife worked – I needed money to bowl and play cards. Virginia was not allowed to even question me, let alone to talk back. It was ten years after our marriage before we were saved: Virginia, our oldest daughter, and me. And guess what? I immediately became a *new creature* and began to treat my wife with the respect she so rightly deserved and took over many of the household chores – no, I did not!

Indeed, my eternal soul was permanently saved from God's judgment and damnation; and I was born again as a spiritual child of God. But humanly, I was the same wretched, macho type I had been all my life. My mind had not been programmed by God's Word yet. It would be another ten years before God would deliver me from my anger and disrespect of women. Gradually throughout that ten years, I would look for ways I could help Virginia in the natural course of life. I found that it was okay to go to the kitchen and pour my own drink or get a snack, something I would not have done before – women's work you know. Now, when I missed the trash with my dirty tissue, I picked it up. I also began picking up after myself: dirty clothes, tools, projects. Virginia has had the joy of finding that these changes were not just physical but in my attitude as well. Now I try to let her know in both action and words that I truly cherish her. I am not perfect. Trained behavior is difficult to eradicate, but it can be controlled somewhat. With God's Spirit, self-discipline can be attained. At least I know what wrong behavior is now.

Emasculated or Effeminate Males As Children

(Again, we are still studying little boys who have been overly influenced by well-meaning females while deserted by their fathers.) Emasculated and effeminate males are at the other extreme pole from the macho males. These are the compliant little boys who desire to please mother, or any other female caregiver. They are generally nice and socialize well with girls and other similarly disposed boys. Such a boy's mother may be sharply critical and/or controlling. His father will not likely have been a major influence toward masculinity in his life, either because of being absent or emasculated himself. Mothers and teachers love this type of boy because he is no trouble (not disobedient), he is helpful around the house, generally does well in academics, and doesn't even get dirty often. He can be easily manipulated by his mother by withholding approval, or by telling him that he has disappointed her, or that she is "so" ashamed of him. My generation (The Silent Generation) was not too kind to momma's boys and constantly challenged them to become one of the regular boys, or else. Note: before you get ahead, sissies and shy boys do not necessarily turn out to be homosexuals). Of course, genetics and hormones play a part in the masculinity/femininity of our children. However, homosexuality, like alcoholism is a *choice*, never a predetermined course of action. Science has not found any "homosexual gene" (more on this later).

Fathers *must* take an active role in working with their boys in order for them to become real men. It is not necessary to take them on a hunting or fishing trip every weekend. More important is the *amount of time* and a variety of circumstances in which they are able to see you function in a manly fashion. (Psychology's pacifier for too-busy parents, "It is not the amount of time, but the quality of time" is just more unsubstantiated psycho-babble to discard.) Every trip to obtain auto repairs, to a hardware store, or even to the grocery store is an opportunity to train boys. Let them see how you handle a miss-figured bill, a bad repair job, a needed part not ready when you ordered it, or help Mom out with an errand, etc. Some monitoring of the mother/son relationship may also be needed, especially if she has been overly protective and controlling of the boys. All boys, but especially such a boy, needs to sit under a strong male Bible teacher. It could even be you. He needs to learn that Christianity is not a woman's religion. No more dropping him or your daughter(s) off at the church of their choice. As leader of the family, *you* are the one to select a church on the basis of its loyalty to the Word of God and then be the example of a consistent learner yourself.

This type of boy, left to himself to mature, will probably not choose competitive athletics, contests, or rough play (of course Dad can encourage his son). However, he is much more likely to enjoy artistic hobbies, drama, and academics. This is not bad in and of itself. Good parenting means to train up a well-balanced, complete young person. Parents should never try to make a child into their image. He or she should be encouraged to discover God's purpose for their life and then to follow that path. A father does not need to be disappointed if his son would rather be a teacher than join the marines. Be advised that children seldom emulate their parents (unless it is for bad habits).

Non-Masculine Males As Adults

As a man, a less than masculine male can be successful in a variety of employments. He can do well in the service industry, as a technician, in health care, teaching school, or many subordinate functions from bank teller to computer programmer. Some are good salesmen or politicians. However, he will not likely be very comfortable in a leadership position, especially if there is any pressure or personnel conflict.

As a family man the non-masculine man is usually a deficient leader for the children and the wife. He will probably expect his wife to work in order to share the family's financial burden, and to care for the household finances (control the money, pay the bills, decide on purchases). He may also lean on her for emotional support – to act like his mother (baby him when ill, injured, or suffer a loss) and to share accountability for all decisions which he insists be jointly made. Effeminate type males will normally be shy, or at least quiet, making passive husbands who may unfairly expect their wives to know what they need or want without communication.

Some television characterizations of non-masculine males have been, Dagwood Bumstead and Al Borland (*Home Improvement*). Whining over their loss of control of a situation and accepting the ruling authority of their wife or mother were their most consistent traits. I can still hear Dagwood say, "Aw, gee whiz Blondie, why not?" and Al say, "Tim, you really shouldn't make fun of me like that," each said in a pathetic whiny voice. As I mentioned in the Introduction, Tim Taylor (*Home Improvement*) often portrays a non-masculine male who is controlled by his wife, at least externally, while he remains angry about it on the inside and complains to others. He also plays the macho male any time his masculinity is challenged by any other man – even his own sons. Most of us are simply one extreme or the other, wishing we could be wise, balanced, kind, and admired as was Robert Young (the father in the highly popular 1950's show, *Father Knows Best*). I have been told by some of the children from the generation who watched this program, that the father portrayed on this show (and which type they longed for) was nothing like their own. Many of these youngsters felt cheated.

Of course to have two extremes we must have an "in between." Not every boy is macho male, and not every boy is totally non-masculine. Most children lie somewhere along the line between these two extremes. However, in this day and age, most boys tend to be toward the non-masculine side of the spectrum. Fathers should objectively evaluate their boys *and their selves* to determine if any deficiencies exist. May God open your eyes for this determination and strengthen your character to handle any corrective actions needed. Remember. God does not intend for us to remain in our sins. He intends that we *all* are changed into the image of his son, Jesus Christ. And, He gives us the knowledge and power to do just that.

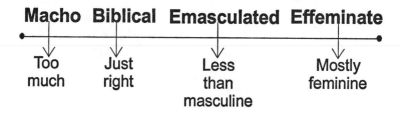

Figure 4.2 Masculinity Scale

2 Corinthians 4:4a *In whom the god of this world hath blinded the minds of them which believe not,*

2 Corinthians 11:3 *But I fear, lest by any means, as the serpent beguiled Eve through his subtlety, so your minds should be corrupted from the simplicity that is in Christ.*

Revelation 12:9a *And the great dragon was cast out, that old serpent, called the Devil, and Satan, which deceiveth the whole world:*

CHAPTER FIVE

SATAN'S ATTACK AGAINST THE FAMILY

Satan has been attempting to destroy the family unit since the Garden of Eden (*What, therefore, God hath joined together, let not man put asunder*, Matthew 19:5,6; Genesis 3:1-5). After Satan deceived Eve into disobeying God, Adam knowingly followed her lead into the sin which ruined all of mankind. Satan must have thought he had successfully destroyed God's institution of marriage and all of mankind in one shot (Genesis 3:6-13). But he was wrong as usual.

Satan continued his attack against God's family from the Garden until the very death of Christ on the cross. He induced the second son of Adam and Eve, Cain, to murder their first son, Abel (Genesis 4); he then attempted to defile the entire human race by infiltrating his fallen angels with mankind (Genesis 6:1-7); and God did indeed destroy all humans except for the eight in Noah's family (Genesis

6-8); again, he tried to get God to wipe out mankind for their disobedience in building the tower of Babel (Genesis 11). Throughout ancient history Satan continued his attack against the seed of Adam, Seth, Noah, Shem, Abraham, Isaac, and Jacob (Israel) – always attempting to block the Seed, Jesus Christ, whom he was told by God would mortally wound him (Genesis 3:15). He tried to destroy either the individual in the bloodline, his marriage, or even the whole nation of Israel. In his attempts over hundreds of years he has used warfare, slavery, and dispersion against Israel. Yes, Satan is obsessive. One of the principles of evil is that it must triumph over good in order to eliminate the contrast for anyone to see.

Now that Christ has come, one might think that Satan's war would be over. But he just keeps fighting like a tantrum-controlled, two-year-old child who doesn't want to go to sleep. He still angrily persecutes the nation of Israel and tries to bring down all of God's ordained institutions: government, marriage, parents, and the true Christian church. Since these are the powers that provide stability and order to the human race, perhaps Satan thinks he can prevent some people from accepting God's plan for salvation if these powers could be destroyed. For example: can you imagine how difficult it is for the children of broken marriages to trust in the love of a God they cannot see, when the father who they could see has abandoned them. And, why would young adults marry and commit to each other for a lifetime when their role-model parents did not.

Maybe Satan even imagined that by dismantling all of God's institutions and making himself the world ruler, he could successfully oppose God's plan to end his evil rule over mankind (Matthew 4:8-9; 1 Corinthians 15:24-26).

He has tried this strategy several times in the past by warfare (Khan, Hitler, etc.) and is now working on a more clever plan – a world government with its own unconquerable military. All he has to do is bring the rulers of all the nations together so he can rule from a single location (Revelation 20:8).

As far as the rest of God's institutions are concerned, Satan has a plan for them also. I believe he is presently attempting to dismantle the Church through ecumenicalism (homogenized doctrine) and humanism (man as god). I also believe he is actively trying to destroy Biblical man and woman (and thereby marriage) through pornography, romanticism, homosexuality, the various feminist's movements, and the destruction of all true masculinity. Finally, I believe he is trying to destroy effective parenting by the false teaching of humanistic child psychology, illegal government intervention of parental rights, unsubstantiated claims of child abuse, non-existent children's rights, and the elimination of corporal punishment. But for now, let us see how Satan is doing on his plan to destroy the family.

Satan's Attack Against Men and Procreation

It has not only been the matriarchal influence and the patriarchal abandonment of America's little boys that have accounted for the demise in men's character today. Satan has also assured the reaching of his objectives by actively promoting his humanistic philosophies throughout the past fifty years. America's people first prepared their hearts for the lies by turning away from learning and living according to God's Word. Then, they turned to science and the false science of psychology for their guidance;

and Satan supplied all of the false information they wanted:

Colossians 2:8 *Beware lest any man spoil you through philosophy and vain deceit, after the tradition of men, after the rudiments of the world, and not after Christ.* (See also 2 Corinthians 4:4; Ephesians 6:12; 2 Timothy 2:26; Revelation 12:3,9a.)

Approximately every ten years from the 1950's on men, women, and children have been subjected to one after another of Satan's evil philosophies. (Actually, the seed for these malevolent thoughts were planted much earlier in history. However, the following chronology indicates the decade in which each of these philosophies generally gained national acceptance and/or legal protection in America. Please study the descriptions given later in this chapter for a more complete explanation of each):

1. 1950's Hedonism – the attack on men's predominant area of weakness, sexual lust.

2. 1960's Drugs and free sex – destruction of the minds and souls of a decade of young people, leading to their total despair.

3. 1970's Women's Liberation Movement – down with normal marriage and God's command to... *be fruitful and multiply.*

4. 1980's The Homosexual Assault – the ultimate destructor of marriage and propagation of children.

Even though society legitimized each of these attacks on the family during the particular decade listed, the impact of each has continued throughout all decades thereafter. Note the following chart:

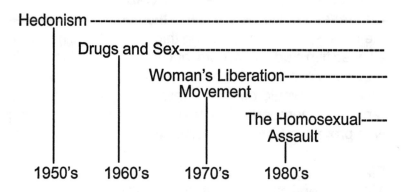

Figure 4.1 Satan's Philosophies Legitimized

We can only surmise if and what comes next; child rights, government rights over all children above three years old, regulation of all religion (state approval), who knows? In ancient history, Satan enticed men and women to sacrifice their own children *by fire* to an idol for their sadistic orgies (Leviticus18:21; 20:2; Jeremiah 32:35; etc.). Maybe in the future an even more depraved humanity than we have now will resort to this practice again. God forbid! We already have abortion and may someday resort to euthanasia of ill and/or unwanted parents or other aged people. Can there be more?

Descriptions

1. HEDONISM – During the 1950's, several Supreme Court decisions (like Burstyn in 1952 and Roth in 1957) opened the floodgates for pornography in America. Playboy magazine led the barrage of smut, followed by the publishing of several previously banned books, and by motion pictures that became increasingly more and more tasteless until this very day. (The Mickey Spillane novels, *Tropic of Cancer* and *Capricorn*, and *Lady Chatterley's Lover* were a few of the books that exercised their free speech of filth during this period.) The new laws allowed film studios, authors, and artists to produce works previously considered to be in bad taste, obscene, or even anti-God. It would only be a few short years before the rankest of pornographers realized that virtually nothing was protected from public display.

Playboy magazine published its first issue in December 1953. Several other magazines exposed themselves over the next forty years. The film, *The Moon Is Blue*, tried the laws and public reaction with previously unheard of racy dialogue. Kinsey's research produced a book, *Sexual Behavior in the Human Female*, supposedly exposing all of women's sexual secrets (at least women who had the lack of personal morals not to mind baring all of their most intimate thoughts and actions to strangers).

Ten years later, Hugh Hefner, founder of Playboy, wrote an argument for hedonism as a right and lifestyle. His philosophy was published in twenty-four brilliantly and logically written articles from December, 1962 to May, 1966. I do not think Satan could have written them any better. Mr. Hefner's philosophy taught that conventional marriage was an unnecessary religious ritual and that traditional morality was bondage. He sold the lies, "if it feels good do it" and, "the only requirement for sex is consenting adults." His attitude toward women is indicated by the macho 'wolf' mascot he originally planned to use (an appropriate symbol for the lecherous stalker of young and unsuspecting women). Since that symbol was already registered, he chose the 'male bunny.' This furry favorite also has obvious sexual characteristics – an insatiable sex drive for innumerable partners, like a playboy. Mr. Hefner's philosophy condoned homosexual, group, and other forms of deviant sexual behavior. Of course, not every boy or man could read, let alone understand, Mr. Hefner's writings. They just looked at the pictures and cartoons. Satan had something else especially for them. Special, graphically-exciting movies hit the screens in 1962 that even the dullest male could understand. These movies all had the same formula:

A. The male hero was a worldly, sophisticated, macho man who could seduce even the most beautiful and desirable woman within seconds, use her sexually without giving any commitment, discard her, and go on to the next one – like a bunny.

B. The women were all beautiful, normally clad in sexually stimulating clothing or less, had no morals, and also required no commitment from the hero.

C. The stories were high adventure, exciting, and the hero always had lots of money. He could engage in every sensuous activity he wished – high-speed rides in or on cars, boats, planes, skis, snowmobiles, parachutes, jet skies, mini-subs, etc. Of course he could also gamble for huge stakes – and win! A playboy's dream come true – women, excitement unlimited, and wealth – non-stop hedonism. How could most young men not want to be like one of these favorite heroes?

These movies were the James Bond, Our Man Flint, Matt Helm, and other various imitators. To visualize this attack on males, notice the blitzkrieg of just some of the movie releases below:

Bond	Flint (James Coburn)	Matt Helm (Dean Martin)	& Others
1962			
1963			
1964			
1965	1966	1966(2)	
1967	1967	1967	
1969			
1971			
1973 (and every two years or so thereafter)			

Figure 4.2 Movie Release Dates for The Heroes of Hedonism

By 1973 almost every man in America under thirty years old had been indoctrinated by the 'rabbit' philosophy. After ten years or so of this intense brainwashing, it is surprising that any men bothered to get married. Even when they did, many would treat their wives as they thought their macho hero might have done. No cherishing love for the weaker vessel; no unconditional covenant; no concern about her protection, provision, or leadership. The effects of undermining the dignity of womanhood in this time period continues to this day. And... Satan smiles.

The impact of fifty years of hedonism has been our people's disintegrating standards of morality resulting in low class speech, dress, thinking, and attitudes. Women today use words and openly express ideas that would have been obscene in previous times. Mothers often dress in clothing better suited to a prostitute. Men today use speech in front of ladies not fit for a drunken sailor. The movies of today use profane, gutter language of the streets and we have to install language blockers to protect our children. Everyone operates on the principal that what they want is the most important if not the only thing that matters.

2. DRUGS AND FREE SEX – as if promoting sexual permissiveness in men was not enough, the next attack was originally aimed at boys and girls of college age. The battle cry was, "Tune in, turn on, and drop out," heralded by Dr. Timothy Leary, self-appointed Pied Piper to this generation of young people. "Tune in" meant, *listen to me*; "turn on" meant, *to take mind-altering drugs* (marijuana, methadone, L.S.D., or cocaine); "drop out" meant, *to quit trying to fit into society.* This meant to drop out of college, do not plan a career, do not do anything that perpetuates the old order – government, military, family, church, Wall Street, or orderly society. The result of drugs plus the emotional desire of these young people for a family closeness most of them had never experienced (where love was unconditional and equal for everyone), was the hippy culture. Indiscriminate sexual experimentation was substituted for true love (concern for the benefit of the one person of the opposite sex who had been identified as your lifelong mate).

Drugs were seen as a way of experiencing the inner self (and even God) in a totally non-traditional way. Psychedelic trips were not just to forget the problems of life (like alcohol was) but a way of "finding yourself," or of discovering God, or a hidden meaning of life. These youngsters literally gave over their wills to drugs. They lost all purpose and meaning for life except for some meaningless sayings like "being there," i.e. implying that one had experienced a trip he recommends but cannot explain. Existential philosophy (no absolutes, just make up the rules as you go) was put into practice by this dream-warped generation – many of whom could not tell reality from fantasy even when they were not high. Without purpose or rational thinking, these children were easy to manipulate and lead around. Dr. Leary, Jerry Rubin, the Chicago Seven, the Black Panthers, Charles Manson, Allen Ginsberg, and other leaders used these youngsters as cannon fodder for their own political agendas. They were summoned to causes such as Kent State, the Berkeley riots, the Chicago Democratic convention, civil rights marches, numerous anti-war marches (remember: "better red than dead" and " make love, not war?"), and anything else they wanted to promote. The bohemian lifestyle hippies advocated neither produced stable families nor well-trained children. The events of this decade tore at the fabric of America's character and politics. And... Satan laughed.

Many anti-society youths eventually "found themselves" and turned toward evangelical, conservative leadership, finished their college educations, or started sole-proprietor businesses that became successful. Of course their lives were scarred, mostly due to the indiscriminate sexual experiences which had seared their souls. Men of this decade would have had a difficult time in cherishing their wives. They would also have great difficulty in training their children in proper character – honesty, self-discipline, loyalty, personal accountability, consideration for others above self – not having developed many of these characteristics themselves. Some of these men and women seriously began a search for truth in every area of their lives. (Most of the readers of this book were raised by parents of this decade.)

Forty or so years after the drug and free sex counterculture had programmed two decades of our youth, America is still feeling the impact. These untrained children became the parents of the young people of the 1980's and 1990's. Considering that only 20 to 25% of those marriages lasted, it is little wonder that their children were also not properly trained.

3. WOMEN'S LIBERATION MOVEMENT – this is now called, The Feminist Movement, of which there have been active proponents for over 100 years (Ms's. Anthony, Stanton, Stone, and Willards, to name a few).

This movement became a full-blown force during the 1970's as women took to the streets, marching for equality with men and total freedom from God's order in marriage and in his institutions. The leaders of this movement have almost all been single, militantly anti-male, sometimes lesbian (or at least have always supported the lesbian lifestyle of their sisters) – but not supporters of the lifestyle of Biblically-ordered marriages. They promote girls remaining single, pursuing a career, and only marrying as an equal business relationship. The development of 'the pill' contraceptive freed women for irresponsible sex just like men. Abortion upon demand has always been promoted by the women's movement worldwide. In 1965 all 50 states had laws banning abortion, but by 1973 the Supreme Court made those laws illegal with their Roe vs. Wade decision. The effective result was that abortion became a 'right' in all 50 states. To give the woman even more power and freedom, no-fault divorces became legal in the 1980's and could be used either by a husband or wife.

So what is the bottom line? If the woman doesn't marry, or dissolves her existing marriage; if she prevents all pregnancies, or terminates them by abortion; the family is mortally wounded, if not destroyed. Do you think Satan supports this on-going movement? Absolutely, and Satan is delighted!

Thirty solid years of women's liberation have resulted in more divorces, more dissatisfaction, and more unhappiness than ever before in America's history for millions of families. However, women now get to work on road gangs, for construction companies, and in any other nasty job a man previously sweated out a living.

4. THE HOMOSEXUAL ASSAULT – mankind has always faced the problem of aberrant sexual behavior. This problem is not a disease or a freak of genetics which makes certain men or women desire sexual relations with another member of their own sex (homosexual). It is simply sin – erotic desire based on lust. It is the same lust that tempts a man to desire sex with a young child, a forbidden woman, or even an animal. Like all sin, it is strictly a decision.

The men of Sodom had become totally depraved at the time of Lot's residence there and they desired to force homosexual acts on two strangers (actually angels) who had been invited to Lot's house. God destroyed Sodom and Gomorrah the next day (1868 B.C.) as He had promised beforehand for their sins (Genesis 18:20; 19:24,25). God later set down specific laws against various kinds of sexual perversions in the Mosaic Law of 1462 B.C. He knew mankind would consider: men with men (Leviticus 18:22; 20:13); b) incest (Leviticus 18:6–18; 20:11); c) man or woman with an animal (Exodus 22:19; Leviticus 18:23); and d) adultery (Deuteronomy 22:25; Leviticus 18:20; 20:10). The punishment for each of these crimes against society was the death penalty.

And how about the New Testament? Did God turn the other cheek and condone homosexuality in His love? I have heard that modern-day homosexuals actually claim the Old Testament curses no longer pertain to them because of the love of Christ. Please read the following verses:

This is one of the clearest and harshest descriptions about the human who *knows* the existence of God, willfully *rejects* His right to rule and to be worshiped, and instead *chooses* to live in defiance against God. The following verses describe God's present-day attitude toward homosexuality in clear terms.

Romans 1: 26-28 *For this cause God gave them up unto vile affections: for even their women did change the natural use into that which is against nature: And likewise also the men, leaving the natural use of the woman, burned in their lust one toward another; men with men working that which is unseemly, and receiving in themselves that recompense of their error which was meet. And even as they did not like to retain God in their knowledge, God gave them over to a reprobate mind, to do those things which are not convenient;*

These passages do not indicate that a person having committed a homosexual act is any more beyond salvation than anyone else, but they do say that a person who rejects the revealed knowledge of God (his character and godliness) may be turned over to an obsession for this perverted lifestyle.

Throughout history there have always been some men and a few women who have developed a sexual lust for members of the same sex. Members of the nobility, the very wealthy, those bored with a normal life style, and those whose senses have been dulled by over-stimulation have been the most likely to be tempted (with artistic temperaments making up the majority of these deviates). However, the lifestyle did not gain acceptance from the time of Sodom and Gomorrah until the 1980's. Even historians sympathetic to homosexuals have difficulty tracing more than random participants to this perversion throughout history. A professor, Paul Halsall, has listed about 1000 known or reputed homosexuals from Greek times to the current day (2500 years) on his various web pages. It is reported that there were over ten times more homosexuals from 1980 to 1999 than from 1900 to 1949, and three times more than there were from 1950 to 1965.[1] This huge increase is due at least in part to the support of the news media, the entertainment industry, and our politicians' change in morality by the 1980's. (Could this be our untrained Boomer generation in action?) I suggest that the destruction of the family unit and lack of moral training of our children during the past fifty years has also contributed to the ranks.

Our country has truly "come a long way, baby." It has come all the way from having laws in almost all 50 states against homosexual acts (under the name of sodomy) prior to the 1960's; to public tolerance, or at least acquiescence, in the 1980's. The "queers" of the past became the "gays" of the Gay Rights Movement (as they were publicized ever since the Stonewall Riot, June 29,1969). Public acceptance greatly improved through the television show, *Soap* (1977 - 1981), and the part played by Billy Crystal as a boy who just 'happened' to be born queer and who had hundreds of homosexual jokes to make everyone laugh. This technique has often been used to make a wrong seem acceptable – what you laugh at today, you will accept tomorrow.

The first gay rights March on Washington occurred in 1979. In 1982 Wisconsin had the honor of passing the first Gay Rights bill. Homosexuals and their supporters marched on Washington again in 1993 – this time reportedly with one million people. The military soon after changed its policy on homosexuals in the service and adopted "don't ask, don't tell " as its new policy. This was also the same year the Clinton Administration appointed the openly gay, Roberta Achtenberg, as assistant Secretary of HUD. Homosexuals are now considered a legitimate minority by our government and by federal law. This may eventually produce affirmative action cases as to how many homosexuals a business owner must hire. Our country has become almost completely decadent. Has Satan already won? May God forbid! But, I do think he is hilariously happy at man's stupidity.

Twenty years of homosexual acceptance by our government and our overly-tolerant people have promoted this ungodly sin to a badge of honor. AIDS and other sexually transmitted diseases are only the physical results. The consequences to the soul and the spirit may never be known.

Conclusion

In just fifty years, America's people (with Satan's able assistance to be sure) have unraveled the moral fabric of a once great nation and taken it precariously close to destruction.

Men have abdicated their God-designed roles as father/trainer of their children; and husband/leader, provider, protector, cherisher of their wives.

Women have succumbed to the siren's false message of freedom without responsibility and have abandoned their God-designed role as mother/teacher, nurturer of her children; and wife/companion, assistant, partner to their husbands.

Children today have little hope for their future. Convinced they are the non personal, non important accident of evolution living in a dying world where soon there will not be enough water, air, food, and even land for them all; not being truly loved and trained into adulthood by their birth-parents; they feel lost and alone.

Drugs, the occult, fulfillment of personal lusts, even suicide seem reasonable alternatives to escape from this hopelessness. Hedonism, free love and sex, women's liberation, and homosexuality will continue to be the lifestyle for the next generations *unless* we turn to God and His way of life for mankind.

And, it starts with you!

Note

1. *Journal of the History of Sexuality,* internet article by Professor Paul Halsall.

Isaiah 5:20 *Woe unto them that call evil good, and good evil; that put darkness for light, and light for darkness; that put bitter for sweet, and sweet for bitter!*

1Thessalonians 5:22 *Abstain from all appearance of evil.*

SECTION ONE CONCLUSION

We are finally through with our sociology/history study. The undeveloped male may now think he has learned all of the excuses he could ever want for continuing to be an immature man. Perhaps his own dad (probably himself untrained) was not 'there' for him (whose was?); maybe his mom was overbearing and controlling (in his teens she also could have been critical and nagging); finally, he could have been discouraged by years of other caregivers belittling him for his boyish behavior and slowness in academics. He has also been affected by the feminists' propaganda as it has reinforced any warped feelings toward women he acquired during his childhood.

As a result of these negative influences, he may not be the man he wishes he was. He may disrespect or even hate womankind. No off-balance member of manhood (one who either detests women or is intimidated by them) makes a good husband or father. If you are a man who has allowed experiences and/or Satan's deceptions, as has been set forth in this section, to affect you negatively, *you can be set free*. First, you must come to understand what has affected you. Doctors cannot give a poisoned patient an antidote until they know what kind of poison he has received and how much. You are already well on your way to discovering the type of poison you have swallowed, but before you can take the cure you will need to know yourself better and the type of antidote required. Physically, a man can escape from a prison camp by the use of his brain and brawn. But the man who has been affected by any of the factors previously covered has his soul in a prison which can only be escaped from by the power of God. There is hope for you, and maybe even our country, but you will have to commit yourself to the study of God's Word and to being conformed to its teaching.

Romans 12:1-2 *I beseech you therefore, brethren, by the mercies of God, that ye present your bodies a living sacrifice, holy, acceptable unto God, which is your reasonable service. And be not conformed to this world: but be ye transformed by the renewing of your mind, that ye may prove what is that good, and acceptable, and perfect, will of God.*

Our next section will deal with who you really are. We will study God's creation of the species He called mankind – *male and female made he them.* Then, we will explore the differences between man and woman and see the unique roles for which they were designed by God. Be assured, you will know yourself better after this section.

SECTION TWO

THE MAKE-UP OF MAN'S SOUL –
WHO AM I?

Creation and the Differences
Between Men and Women

Jeremiah 31: 29-30 *In those days they shall say no more, The fathers have eaten a sour grape, and the children's teeth are set on edge. But every one shall die for his own iniquity: every man that eateth the sour grape, his teeth shall be set on edge.*

CHAPTER SIX

LIKE FATHER, LIKE SON?

What makes us the way we are? Genes make up our physical being – shape of nose, color of eyes, amount of hair, overall size, every little detail. They are the basic units of heredity – a direct link to our ancestors. But, what about our soul?

What 'causes' a person to become a hero, or a criminal, or an all-around average person? What makes a person become a Ted Bundy, a Fidel Castro, or an Osama Bin Laden? What factors make up a hero or a truly great person? Psychologists have been attempting to answer this question ever since psychology invented itself about 150 years ago. It has set forth various theories about why people turn out the way they do. Sigmund Freud, Carl Jung, Alfred Adler, Carl Rogers, Abraham Maslow, William Glasser, Thomas Harris, and their many devotees credit one or more of the following influences as the source of man's soul development:

HEREDITY. Science has found no gene that produces either a 'bad seed' or 'good' people. However, the four-generation curse of Proverbs and the Ten Commandments indicate that God will allow an innate drive to reject Him for up to four generations – (Exodus 20:5,6; Proverbs 30:11-14.) [1]

ENVIRONMENT. The home life in which one is raised. This includes the quality of parenting; the type of peer, school, and church influences; as well as any atmosphere of crime, poverty, or depravity with which one is raised.

LIFE EXPERIENCES. The effect of catastrophic events in a child's life, such as the early death of a parent, their divorce, his permanent injury, frequent relocating, or his failures before peers.

EDUCATION. Social engineers have always believed they could eliminate most of man's problems by educating everyone from early childhood to think and feel the same way they do about social, political, and religious issues. Those in the religion of Psychology consider any child who misses this 'fine' education to be handicapped, especially if he has been educated by his parents. If a child has also been taught religious values, he can be considered abused and possibly antisocial. [2]

The Human Will

In reality, none of psychology's supposed 'causes' for the soul problems of man is a satisfactory answer. These theories assume a one-to-one correlation between cause and effect. But, God has granted every man the will to choose how and to what extent outside pressures may affect him. Therefore, even though it is true that each of us has been influenced by what our parents have done (...*the children's teeth are set on edge*), or the challenges life has had for us, God holds us accountable for how we allow things to affect us (*But every one shall die for his own iniquity: every man that eateth the sour grape, his teeth shall be set on edge* – Jeremiah 31:30).

Booker T. Washington, and thousands of other examples, have pulled themselves up from the depths of poor environment, discouraging life experiences, and/or lack of education to become outstanding people. While the above theories can be used as excuses, only a mentally deficient person (one who would truly not be accountable) could be 'conditioned' (or programmed) by these factors. From God's point of view, all other people have a choice and therefore are accountable. The bottom line is that:

Heredity can influence you. Your parents' physiological problems may have handicapped you (the child of an alcoholic or drug-addicted parent is highly likely to become addicted himself – but he can break the addiction and not follow the pattern). A child can be born with a severe deformity, but he *can* overcome any handicap and fulfill God's purpose for his life, unless he chooses to allow that handicap to affect him negatively.

Environment can influence you. Parents, relatives, and others close to you can ridicule, discourage, or even abuse you. Emotional scars can be overcome by those who choose to control their emotions with their mind. Please note that many people have been raised in an optimum environment of loving parents, safety, and security; and still have become rotten in character. External factors do not make us what we are, how we deal with those factors do. *Choices, not environment, determine who we will be.*

Life Experiences can influence you. Bad things that happen to a person tend to scar his emotional being (beyond his ability to make sense of it). These tragedies we may blame on ourselves or even God (It seems to be easier to accept being born without one arm than to lose a limb in an accident). [3]

Education can influence you. The type of education promoted in America since the 1950's definitely handicaps anyone's skill at learning to think and reason for themselves. Today's high school graduate has approximately the same aptitude as an eighth grader in the 1950's – at least in mathematics, grammar, and science. Granted, the boys may be able to sew on a button, and the girls may be able to change a tire; but neither will have been required to think analytically or rationally. The 'education' that has been exchanged for academics by the social engineers is indeed a 'cause' for many of man's problems today. It can be avoided or overcome by taking children out of public education as young as possible (*all* children). Adults will have to start over and re-educate themselves to overcome the damage, as many Christians have already done.

Conclusion

Everyone was born with some kind of physical imperfection, or has lived in a less than perfect family or social environment, or has personally experienced emotional scaring. Like the old saying, "You've got two left feet, your clothes are all torn and dirty, and besides that ... you're ugly." The question is: what are *you* going to do about your problems?

God's Word counsels us to accept the circumstances of life as He allows them to come, *Let your conversation be without covetousness; and be content with such things as ye have:* (Hebrews 13:5); and, *For we brought nothing into this world, and it is certain we can carry nothing out. And having food and raiment let us be therewith content.* (1Timothy 6:7,8). The pressures we have faced in life may not be anyone's fault and may even be used by God as a part of His plan (like the beggar who was born blind) *And his disciples asked him, saying, Master, who did sin, this man, or his parents, that he was born blind? Jesus answered, Neither hath this man sinned, nor his parents: but that the works of God should be made manifest in him.* (John 9:2,3).

Most non-Christians are able to cope (make compensations for) their early childhood problems and still function in life; Christians should be able to do much more – to conquer their problems and convert them to God's advantage *For whatsoever is born of God overcometh the world: and this is the victory that overcometh the world, even our faith. Who is he that overcometh the world, but he that believeth that Jesus is the Son of God?* (1John 5: 4,5). (See also Romans 8:37-39.) So, the answer to the question, "What makes us the way we are?" is not what happens to us; but *what we choose to let affect us.*

Notes

1. Dr. Stanton E. Samenow, is author of *Straight Talk About Criminals.* He said in an interview with *Psychotherapy Book News,* July 23, 1998, "The criminals who came from very adverse environments had brothers and sisters who faced the same problems, but most turned out to be responsible people. What impressed me more and more was not the circumstances from which these people come, but how they choose to deal with those circumstances, however bleak." And, " ...but it is the individual who makes the choices at every turn as to how he or she will live."

Children of alcoholic parents are less intoxicated with a given dose of alcohol than the average child and are thus more likely to become alcoholics (Harvard Mental Health Letter, Vol.15, No. 1). (Since these children's bodies are less affected by alcohol, they become used to drinking larger quantities than others and are therefore more likely to develop a dependence on alcohol.) Even though children of alcoholics may have a strong tendency to become alcoholics themselves, no one makes them take the first drink or to continue afterward.

We used to test our children with the questions, "Can anyone else *make* you do anything you do not choose to do?" "What if they threatened you with torture?" "What if they threatened you with death?" "What if they threatened you with the death of your parents?" We were attempting to teach our children to accept total responsibility for their own actions through this exercise. Accountability is one of the cornerstones of maturity.

2. Humanism has been the philosophy behind public education's teacher materials and student textbooks for over fifty years. This is a sampling of that philosophy:

JOHN DEWEY, dedicated humanist, the father of progressive education and once head of Columbia University's Teachers College, stated: "There is no God and there is no soul. Hence, there are no needs for the props of traditional religion. With dogma and creed excluded, then immutable truth is also dead and buried. There is no room for fixed, natural law, or moral absolutes."

CHARLES FRANCIS POTTER, a signer of the *First Humanist Manifesto*, wrote in his book, *Humanism, A New Religion*: "Education is thus a most powerful ally of humanism, and every public school is a school of humanism. What can the theistic Sunday Schools, meeting for an hour once a week, and teaching only a fraction of the children, do to stem the tide of a five-day program of humanistic teaching?" (Page 128.)

JOHN DUNPHY wrote in the January/February 1983 issue of the *Humanist Magazine*: "I am convinced that the battle for humankind's future must be waged and won in the public school classroom by teachers who correctly perceive their role as the proselytizers of a new faith: a religion of humanity that recognizes and respects what theologians call divinity in every human being."

PAUL BRANDWEIN wrote in the *Social Sciences Journal*: "Any child who believes in God is mentally ill."

DR. PIERCE, recent Professor of Education at Harvard University, stated the following in a speech to teachers: "Every child in America entering school at the age of five is mentally ill, because he comes to school with an allegiance toward our elected officials, toward our institutions, toward the preservation of this form of government we have. All of that proves the children are sick, because the truly well individual is one who has rejected all of those things and is what I would call the true international child of the future."

3. If negative life experiences were really an excuse for failure, those men and women who lived through WWI, the Great Depression, and WWII, would have been totally destroyed psychologically. On the contrary, more advancements in science, industry, agriculture, athletics, and medicine were made from 1950 to 2000 than in the rest of history before then! Each of these people could have chosen any of the following options in dealing with the challenges life had presented them:

a) They could whine, feel sorry for themselves, join the soup line, or give up and commit suicide.

b) they could toughen their soul in order to cope with any problem and determined to succeed no matter what it took. (I have known several such older men in my sixty-plus years who made a vow after the depression "That they would never be broke or hungry again – no matter what." Each of these men had utilized greed, lies, ruthlessness, and unscrupulous business practices in order to achieve their own security. They were "self-made" people who thought they had no need of God.)

c) Then there were those who recognized their need for a higher source of power than themselves and trusted in the one, true God. During times of danger and fear many people will turn to God. As it has been said, "There are no atheists in the foxhole." A Judge friend of mine once said in the 1970's, "I was sorry to see the death penalty go, many lost souls came to Christ on death row."

Genesis 1:1,2 *In the beginning God created the heaven and the earth. And the earth was without form, and void;*

John 1:1,3,4 *In the beginning was the Word, and the Word was with God, and the Word was God. All things were made by him; and without him was not any thing made that was made. In him was life; and the life was the light of men.*

CHAPTER SEVEN

THE CREATION OF MANKIND

We cannot understand our function or purpose in life until we first understand how and why God made mankind the species. (Appendix B, located at the back of this book, contains charts and theological studies that further support the conclusions made in this chapter.)

Mankind is unique as a species; a little lower than the angels (Philippians 2:7,8; Hebrews 2:9), but above all of the animals (Genesis 1:26).

> God
>> angels
>>> humans
>>>> fish, fowl, and all living things

Chart 7.1 The Order of Created Beings

God created the unique species, mankind, on a specific day in history, six literal days after the beginning of time as a part of all creation. Christians now have an abundance of scientific proof that the false theory of evolution is just another attack against God's Word (see materials available from *Creation Research Society*, www.creationresource.org, or Post Office Box 8263, St. Joseph, MO 64508-8263; and *The Institute for Creation Research*, www.icr.org, or Post Office Box 2667, El Cajon, California 92021).

The Bible proves by the use of just a single Hebrew word in the next verse that the immaterial essence of mankind was created directly out of nothing, not evolved through any animal (or fish) species:

Genesis1:27 *So God created man in his own image, in the image of God created he him; male and female created he them.*

That one Hebrew word, translated three times in this verse as "created" is *bara*. It means "to create" something out of nothing when used of God's creative acts. It is used for mankind and everything original God brought into existence, such as the heavens and earth in Genesis 1:1 (See also Hebrews 11:3.). [1] God did not monkey around with man's creation. It occurred at the very beginning of all creation (Matthew 19:4; John 1:1-3), not by chance ten, twenty, or "x" million years later. [2]

The Hebrew word translated 'man' in the above verse is *adam* and means 'mankind.' It was not used as a proper name in Old Testament times with the occasional exception of the first member of the adamic species, Adam. (This is similar to the way we refer to all copiers as a "Xerox.") The point is this, most references to adam in the creation account of Genesis should first be considered as meaning 'mankind' generically rather than Adam as a specific person. God referred to the male and female both as being adam in Genesis 1:27; and in Genesis 5:2, He actually called *their* name adam. It is not likely He was referring to a male and a female person, each named Adam:

Genesis 5:2 *Male and female created he them; and blessed them, and called their name Adam, in the day when they were created.*

They Were Made For Each Other

God had stated that mankind's purpose from the very beginning was designed for a husband and wife team: *And God blessed them, and God said unto them, Be fruitful, and multiply, and replenish the earth, and subdue it: and have dominion over the fish of the sea, and over the fowl of the air, and over every living thing that moveth upon the earth.* (Genesis 1:28). Of course "them" refers to the first pair of male and female humans. God also declared that a man needed a mate: *And the LORD God said, It is not good that the man should be alone; I will make him an help meet for him.* (Genesis 2:18). God could have made Adam and Eve simultaneously, but He chose instead to make man first as a completed being; and then to make the woman out of the man. We will see His reasons for this ordering later.

The words of The Man (*ish*), when he first saw The Woman (*ishshah*), suggest that he identified more than a physical counterpart. *This is now bone of my bones, and flesh of my flesh: she shall be called Woman, because she was taken out of Man.* (Genesis 2:23). Where did this reference to flesh come from? God did not say anything about taking any flesh from the man. The words translated flesh in both the Old and the New Testament generally stand for the bodies (meat) of animals and humans. But, technically, they are used to describe physical life as contrasted with spiritual life, *the spirit indeed is willing, but the flesh is weak.* (Matthew 26:41). (See also Romans 8:4; Galatians 4:29 and 5:17.)

When The Man said "flesh of my flesh," it could have meant either of two things: merely an exclamation of his sight identification of a creature that matched himself physically (unlike any of the animals he had named); or he could have been identifying both the body and the immaterial essence (soul) of his counterpart as having originated from himself. (Even non-Christians believe they can identify their soul mates. I also find it interesting that most love sonnets, poems, and songs throughout history describe the longing for, attachment with, and devastation of loss to the human soul in male/female relationships, not to the physical body.) The New Testament passages that mention the creation of Adam and Eve refer to the completed woman, *gune,* originating from the completed man, *aner* (1 Corinthians 11:8). Also see, *For Adam was first formed, then Eve* (1 Timothy 2:13). Neither of these verses suggest that only the physical substance of the woman was extracted from the man, but imply that the whole being of woman came forth from that man.

Mankind Created To Be One

I believe that the creation of mankind is more unique than our theology has previously uncovered. The passage, *So God created man in his own image, in the image of God created he him; male and female created he them.* (Genesis 1:27), does not say that God created a completed man and woman at the same time, each with their own body. "Them" in this passage is more likely a reference to their souls being entwined and then being held in limbo until unique physical bodies were formed for each (See Psalm 139:13-16; Job 31:5; 33:4; Isaiah 49:16). When the body for Adam was made, I believe both the male/female essence was placed into it by God and then the female soul extracted along with the physical materials to make the woman, *And the rib, which the LORD God had taken from man, made he a woman, and brought her unto the man.* (Genesis 2:22); *For Adam was first formed, then Eve.* (1 Timothy 2:13).

No verse of Scripture specifically states that the soul of the first woman was ever a part of the first man, but neither does this theory contradict God's Word. It does match up with certain known facts in genetics and helps us better understand the importance of marriage in relationship to God's plan. (Since you may not have been exposed to this theory before, please see Appendix B for a more complete presentation of this concept.)

Why do I believe this controversial concept is important enough to set forth, even as theory? First, I believe it is truth after studying it for hundreds of hours over a five year period. Second, I believe God considers it important since the marriage union relates to His Son and the body of all Christians:

Ephesians 5:31,32 *For this cause shall a man leave his father and mother, and shall be joined* (glued or welded facing each other) *unto his wife, and they two shall be one flesh. This is a great mystery: but I speak concerning Christ and the church.* (Note added by the author)

The Greek word *megas* translated "great" in the above verse means:
great in external form or appearance.
great in size, weight, extent, measure, and stature.
great in quantity, age, and might.
great in importance, excellence, and value.

If all believers today accepted the importance and permanence God intended our marriages to be, perhaps we would shine forth as testimonies instead of trying to equal the unbelieving world in our unfaithfulness.

God considers the man's identification of the woman and their subsequent union to be a permanent contract between a man and a woman: *Have ye not read, that he which made them at the beginning made them male and female, And said, For this cause shall a man leave father and mother, and shall cleave to his wife: and they twain shall be one flesh?* (Matthew19:4,5). Note that the bond between a man and his wife will be even stronger than the former bond between him and his parents. Also note that the two will become one. This is not merely a reference to sexual union, but to a new state of being – from two into one. Again, "flesh" is not just the physical substance, but also includes the immaterial essence (soul) of a person as well. God's Word then establishes His Will for all marriage unions, *Wherefore they are no more twain, but one flesh. What therefore God hath joined together, let not man put asunder* (Matthew 19:6). PERIOD! God has ordained the institution of marriage and He is seen in this verse as sanctifying each union (literally, a team joined in yoke). He also establishes a prohibition against *anyone* who would separate this soul-bond. I believe the restriction (let not man put asunder) is not only for those other than the couple, but to each of the partners as well. Marriage is not an option with God; it is the means for forming teams of males and females to procreate, conquer the physical universe, and rule all of creation (Genesis1:28).

There are also some scientific reasons to indicate that male and female souls were at one time entwined. We know that men and women both possess the same number of genes. They also *both* possess masculine and feminine hormones. However, men possess a larger amount of androgen (testosterone) hormones while women have smaller amounts; similarly, women possess larger amounts of estrogen and progesterone while men possess smaller amounts. It is as if these hormones had once been separated (like cream from whole milk), leaving the man and woman with unequal parts of each. Hormones play the major role in determining the sex of the embryo, along with the "Y" chromosome of the man which determines male sex. While it is true that in the womb these hormones can produce a girl who is dainty or one who is tomboyish; or a boy who is "all boy" or a softer, more sensitive one; these *personalities* have no known effect on these children's sexuality. The training those children receive can modify their extreme personalities.

In adulthood, boys who have been genetically predisposed toward effeminacy (Those having XXY chromosome instead of XY; or who had an insufficient amount of androgen or testosterone male hormones during fetal development), are likely to show signs of being effeminate. This does not necessarily led to sexual disorientation, only to feminine (less aggressive) characteristics. Likewise, girls born with the kidney disorder called CAH are likely to exhibit masculine (more aggressive) characteristics. [3] There is no scientific proof that anyone is genetically born to be a homosexual. Even if this were true, it would still be a matter of accountability for the individual (see Chapter Six).

You should now have a greater appreciation for your wife and a deeper understanding of the oneness of your souls:

Ephesians 5:28,29 *So ought men to love their wives as their own bodies. He that loveth his wife loveth himself. For no man ever yet hated his own flesh; but nourisheth and cherisheth it, even as the Lord the church.*

How could a Christian man ever desert his own flesh? It would be parallel to Christ deserting The Church. God Forbid! Even if you married your wife for any or all of the wrong reasons, your souls have become entwined. You may both think you cannot stand each other, but there are thousands of testimonies from couples who look back at the place you may now stand. These testimonies range from those who divorced and later realized what they could have had; to those who committed themselves to honor their marriages (even when the each thought they did not love each other), and then became one in reality – *through God's power*. God always honors His commitments. (See Chapter Eleven for the real meaning of love.)

Notes

1. *Commentary on the Old Testament*, by C.F. Keil and F. Delitzsch, William B. Eerdmans Publishing, Co., Grand Rapids, Michigan. Vol. I, Chapter 1.1, p.47 "...in the kal (a Hebrew stem), *bara* always means ' to create,' and is only applied to a divine creation, the production of that which had no existence before."

2. *A Greek Lexicon of the New Testament*, 4th revised ed., by William F. Arndt and F. Wilbur Gingrich, University of Chicago Press, licensed

by Zondervan Publishing House.

p. 111, *arche*, 1. "beginning, origin," (Matthew 19:4; John 1:1,2; 2 Peter 3:4).

p.157, *ginoma*i, 1. "become, originate," 2. "be made, created," (John 1:3).

3. *Brain Sex*, by Anne Moir and David Jessel, Dell Publishing, 1992. Chapter Two, pp. 21-25 & 92; and references on that chapter, pp.209-212

Proverbs 23:7 *For as he thinketh in his heart, so is he:*

CHAPTER EIGHT

THE DIFFERENCES BETWEEN MEN AND WOMEN

It is amazing that we live in a time when it is necessary to prove the natural differences between boys and girls. When I was growing up everyone understood that boys were different from girls. Girls were soft, boys were hard; girls wore dresses (those were long, pieces of billowing material that covered most of a girl's body), and boys wore jeans. Boys played rough and tumble sports, girls played with dolls and talked, and talked, and talked. Even adults of the last few generations have been able to tell men from women.

However, for at least twenty years feminists have been arguing against all scientific proof to the contrary that women are just like men – mentally, emotionally, and even physically. Their battle cry has been, "Women can do anything men can do better." Sadly, many Christian psychologists, pop preachers, and authors have swallowed and promoted this lie. Christian men have been taught that they need to become more understanding, more of a communicator, more sensitive. As a result, men have been made to feel almost guilty just for being a man. Actually, the male who supposes he is a real man just because he is macho, needs to act less like a clod. However, I believe the biggest problem in our nation today is effeminate males who fear the role of leadership over their wives and children. At one large congregation where I taught this message, many men (including the pastor) afterward said, "As Christians they had been trying not to be leaders."

This book will concentrate on setting forth the truth about men and women, not waste your time in proving the fallacy of the feminist lie. Men and women think differently, they communicate differently, they react differently emotionally, and they are different physically. It seems reasonable to conclude that God designed them to be different for a purpose. Understanding the differences in men and women is necessary in order to function properly in your role as man, husband, and father.

The Physical Differences

Throughout mankind's history, women have always been smaller and frailer in physical structure than men. This fact has placed them in jeopardy from attack and harm from evil men, and in need of male protection. A woman is not built for combat. Her major arm muscle is on the back of her arm enabling her to cradle heavy loads (like babies, laundry, and groceries) for long periods of time. By contrast, a man's upper body strength is roughly twice that of a woman's and his biceps muscle contracts rapidly with great force enabling him to lift heavy tools, swing a pick or ax, and to shovel with relative ease. The majority of a man's weight mass is located in his torso while a woman's is in her lower body. These unique physical factors enable a man to do the heavy tasks that need real muscle power; and to protect his family better. The average woman is not built to perform the physically demanding work of a man. God did not make women to compete physically with men; He meant for men to perform the physically demanding work. For thousands of years, men have protected women from doing work beneath the dignity of a lady – serving in the military or police duty, working in physically strenuous or dangerous jobs (logging, working on fishing boats, road and building construction, hunting, etc.).

1 Peter 3:7 *Likewise, ye husbands, dwell with them according to knowledge, giving honour unto the wife, as unto the weaker vessel,*

Women were intentionally made more delicate then men and not designed for these physically demanding types of labor. The fact that some can perform the same duties as men (or a modified, female-handicapped version) is not the point. Women were designed by God to complete the man – to be a companion, helpmate, counterpart – one to help him be successful in his calling (see my wife's book, *VICTORIOUS WOMEN – On the Other Side of the Garden*, for the presentation of the woman's Biblical role).

Genesis 2:18 *And the LORD God said, It is not good that the man should be alone; I will make him an help meet for him.*

Physical Differences of the Brain

The brain is a physical organ of the body that also reveals unique differences between men and women. Since at least the early 1980's, there have been two, totally opposing forces at work concerning the issues of male and female physiological and psychological differences. One force has been the tremendous increase in legitimate scientific research proving the facts concerning the differences between the sexes; the other has been the highly biased, emotional opposition to that research and its overwhelming implications. This emotional onslaught has come from the feminists attempting to apply political and social pressure against any such research or publication of scientific findings. (One leading feminist said she believed that such research should not be allowed because it impedes her cause.) Some researchers have given up their work under this pressure, others have distorted their true findings in order to appease the feminists, and still others actually did lose their research funding.

Are these differences created by God for specific purposes, or do they occur as the feminists claim because of the biased way parents and society raise our children? This should be easy to determine. Much of the recent, scientific research proves male/female brain differences begin in the womb. Every embryo (from its inception through eight weeks) begins life as neither male nor female. If the father has contributed a "Y" chromosome in his sperm to join with the "X" chromosome in the mother's egg, the resulting child will be a boy – if it is further exposed to a sufficient amount of male hormones. (These hormones normally begin to be produced by the embryo itself in the sixth or seventh week after conception.) [1]

Somewhere between the eighteenth and twenty-sixth week, another chemical bath of male hormones washes over the brain of the male fetus (called a fetus from now until birth) and changes it physiologically from the initial brain of a female fetus. This wash causes the right hemisphere (lobe) to recede slightly, and it also diminishes part of the male brain's corpus callosum – the communication linkage between left and right hemispheres. [2,3] With these seemingly minor changes to men's brains, God establishes major differences between the thinking, communication, and emotions of typical men and women. The chart below is an exaggerated depiction of these physiological differences:

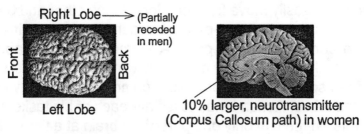

Figure 8.1 Comparison of Male and Female Brains

Now, let us examine the specific functions of the left and right lobes of the human brain: [4]

LEFT HEMISPHERE
(communication lobe)

verbal (mechanics of language)
detailed
practical
concrete thinking
orderly, in sequence, logical

RIGHT HEMISPHERE
(analytical thinking lobe)

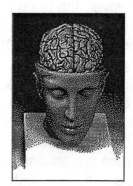

visual
visualizes in gestalt (big picture)
imagines shapes & patterns
uses abstract thought
major emotional center
analytical
has spacial navigational skills

**Figure 8.2 Dominant Brain Functions
in the Left and Right Hemisphere**

Both men and women can utilize either side of their brain. Forget the overly simplistic theories that were popular a few years ago about some people being left-brain thinkers while others were right-brain thinkers; or that men were right-brained while women were left-brained. In reality, women easily move from one lobe to the other and back again across their ten-percent-larger neuro-transmitter – the corpus callosum path. A woman can think about several tasks at once and even verbalize them as she does so. Men have less rapid communication between their lobes. A man tends to isolate each of his tasks and work on them in only one part of his brain at a time. This makes men's and women's methods of thinking different, neither better nor worse. We should view these brain differences as God's ingenious way of making us uniquely fitted for our roles, as we shall soon see.

Enter the Hormones

However, the brain is not the principal factor producing the major differences between men and women. Hormones cause the brain to function in either a masculine or a feminine way. The hormones, testosterone and estrogen, act on the brain to create aggressive tendencies in the male and emotional/nurturing tendencies in the female. We will next consider the specific differences these hormones make on the thinking of men and women. Please understand, as we go through this next section, we are dealing with general tendencies, not all of the possible variations. For example: the fact that men generally are aggressive and that women generally are not, does not mean your boy has to enjoy fighting with other kids; or that your young daughter cannot step in and organize a game for a group of neighborhood boys and girls. It also means there is nothing wrong with a boy who desires reading and art over baseball and Axel grease; or a daughter who chooses horseback riding over playing with dolls.

Many men will identify with the male profile given below. Some men (mostly those under forty years old) have already become emasculated or even somewhat effeminate due to their responses to childhood influences and lack of masculine training. Therefore, they may identify themselves by some of the feminine characteristics as well as not identify with some masculine ones. Study the following list of characteristics below that are scientifically most specific to men and women in general: [5]

Male
aggressive, competitive nature
analytical, logical, linear thinking
spacial tasking (3D)
mathematical reasoning
perception of vertical and horizontal
map reading
targeting ability
single-minded, specialized,
strong concentration, less distractable

Female
verbal fluency
perceptual speed
verbal and item memory
fine motor skills
abstract thought
emotional response
intuitive
interpersonal skills, concern for people and relationships
empathetic, compassionate

Figure 8.3 Masculine and Feminine Personality Traits

Let us examine some of these characteristics in detail:

Communication

Experiments have been conducted with kindergarten children at play to learn how little boys and girls talked. Girls seem to talk almost all the time – either to others around them, their dolls, or themselves. Boys only used words about 68 percent of the time and communicated with various noises the rest of the time. These noises included sounds of their play like the bang of a gun, the varoom of a car, and assorted Batman-type sounds. Another study found that men use about 12,500 words during a day while women use about 25,000 words. Men's purpose in communicating is to make a point, to get to the bottom line –"just the facts, Ma'am."

Women tend to take a trip with their communication, painting pictures as they go and developing character sketches of the people they encounter. Many of a woman's words will be spent in providing a complete story with pictures and dramatizations (especially if the man is silent or ignoring her). Women will often ask as many questions as necessary to visualize a full story around their husband's mini-synopsis type communication. An illustration of this is when a husband might say," I'm going to the store." The wife may want to know which store and then what he was planning to buy. She does not mean to be nosy, just trying to picture the trip. She desires to be a part of her husband's life and make him a part of hers. As she pictures the store and where he will be shopping in the store, she may 'see' something in her mind needed for the home that he could easily pick up. Asking questions is where a lot of those 25,000 words go each day.

Women have the ability to perceive thoughts faster than men and the verbal fluency to say those thoughts with great rapidity. They can unintentionally intimidate most men with their verbal acuity, rapid ability to think in multiple sections of their brain simultaneously, and strong emotional passion. Most men admit that they fear, or at least try to avoid, their wife's tongue. Women can also be thinking and talking about multiple subjects sequentially or even simultaneously. Their minds are intuitive and capable of abstract thought. The minute a man is late coming home or changes his routine in some way, his wife is likely to begin imagining things. She may imagine an accident or another woman (her thoughts will probably not be anything too flattering since they will be powered by her emotions). This is one reason why men need to be careful in explaining their activities to their wives.

Leadership

God has commanded men to be the heads of their families; about which we will study more thoroughly later (See Genesis 3:16; 1 Corinthians 11:3; Ephesians 5:23, 24; 1 Timothy 3:2-5,12). Men have the drive and ability to be leaders due to their long-range vision, objective orientation, and proclivity to plan. A leader understands that some decisions in life must be made that results in pain and/or sacrifice for today in order to accomplish what is right or best in the future. (Like chastising a child, overcoming fear in order to defend his family or his country, or enduring physical pain or an abusive boss.) Where a man's emotions might introduce doubts about his ability to lead, objective thinking and the more assertive characteristics of his brain aid him in overcoming such reservations.

A man's thinking is slower, deliberate, analytical, logical (less emotional), less distracted, and single-minded. Analytical thinking enables a man to make good decisions even beyond the availability of the facts. He is not likely to get bogged down in details or distracted from reaching his objective. As an example, when a man considers purchasing a home, he usually looks at whether he can handle the financing, the insurance, and the maintenance. Later, when his wife asks him away from the house if he liked the color of the drapes, he is likely to say, "What drapes?" He is not likely to allow temporary problems at home (minor child training issues, unresolved family plans, or non-threatening home repairs) to prevent him from meeting his employment responsibilities. While men are normally goal-oriented, women are more maintenance-oriented. Men are visionaries; women attend to the details of the vision.

Each party needs to understand these differences and communicate in a way that is compatible with the other. Why do men and women think so differently? Because God made us to be two, distinctly unique beings in order to fulfill our separate roles.

Competitiveness and Aggressiveness

Men tend to be assertive, practical, competitive, achievement driven (every game must have a winner); they are willing to endure the personal sacrifice of time, comfort, health, relaxation, or safety to achieve their ambitions. From childhood they have explored, tested, and challenged things in their world in order to discover their parameters and fulfill their egos (personal identities). They learn to express themselves as being self-confident and self-reliant. The masculine man is a risk-taker and a conqueror. To him investments should produce profits. Competition is even an element of a man's protectiveness over his wife and family. He is ever alert to the fact another man would steal what is his and this fact abets his drive to protect his family. Competition is also a key element of a man's drive to provide for his family. When a man becomes effeminate, his competitiveness is stunted and relationships become more important than personal achievement. However, a masculine man is driven to succeed. Such a man will look for ways to plant better crops, advance in his job, or build a better mousetrap. Without the character of competitiveness he would be less able to provide well for his family.

Similarly, aggressiveness makes man a perfect candidate for being a protector and provider for his wife and children. Even at an early age a boy will respond quite seriously to the idea of being 'the man of the house' while Daddy is away. Girls seldom have this inclination. A man's proper ego is defined by his aggressive and competitive character. Manliness (a healthy male ego as designed by God) is an important component of a man's stability. It is the part of a man that gives him the courage to be a leader for his family. Competitiveness and aggression go hand-in-hand. They prompt a man to compete in sports, business, and for the hand of his bride.

Feminists have always ridiculed any part of a man's character that seems exclusively male or macho to them. Women need to be aware that a man's drive to achieve and his competitiveness contributes to his providing for the family; and that his aggressiveness is where he draws the courage to fight for her and the children's protection.

Women are satisfied just to participate in the games and share the moment rather than have to win. They prefer not to take risks. Investments to them are a means to preserve principle and to maintain security. Otherwise, women are loving, affectionate, impulsive, generous, and nurturing beings. [6,7] Women think about the details of issues and the more immediate short-range viewpoint. They are concerned more with building and nourishing relationships than reaching objectives. Men see people as co-workers – if they are not willing to pitch in and help get the job done, what good are they? Women look to people for companionship and friendship and are usually the ones who remember to buy and mail birthday and thank-you cards. They notice moods, the tone of voice, and facial expressions of those around them. While men hear the literal words that someone speaks, women hear the meaning that a whole person speaks. Such wordless language tells them when others are upset or need help. Women are much more emotional than men due to having several more emotion centers in their brains and being exposed to entirely different hormones both in the womb and throughout their lives. Environment and training in childhood obviously does not create these differences as the Feminists claim.

Character Development

But are not all of these previously mentioned male/female behaviors trained into children by their parents and other adults? Those who market toys to children research the boy/girl issue intensely. They realize that if they could make a unisex toy, their profits would go up immensely. But the simple fact is that by five or six years old, children have already developed noticeably different masculine/feminine behavior patterns:

- boys exhibit aggression while girls do not.
- boys thrive on risk-taking, problem-solving, competition, and desire for independence.
- boys desire games that are goal-oriented, physical, and 'outward' – like king-of-the-hill and wrestling
- boys play is harsher, object-centered with sports and other action-figured toys, and dangerous themes such as monsters and battles.

- girls desire play that is more nurturing, cooperative, creative, expressive, and 'inward.'
- girls play is gentler, relationship-centered, safe, and home-like.

Some successful crossover games and toys have been found – virtual pets, certain board games, and some fashion items. But, the manufacturer who tries to force little boys to play with dolls and doll clothes, sewing and needlepoint kits, or plush toys; or little girls to play with toy trucks and trains, play guns, action and super-hero figures is looking for financial suicide. Of course, if a boy finds himself at a doctor's office surrounded by girl-toys, he may play with them – such as pile the dolls into a make-believe fort and throw toy dishes as bombs at its walls. Many a doll's leg has simulated a gun in a boy's hand. [8]

Boys and girls exhibit their differences even as babies:

- Female babies only a few hours old are much more sensitive to tactile stimulation than males. They are also less tolerant to loud noises and become irritated or hurt by it.

- Female babies (two-to four-days old) make eye contact with adults entering their room for twice as long as the males. Females immediately begin to gurgle at visitors; males are just as happy jabbering at an abstract mobile over their cribs. Females are born with a bias for people while males have a bias for things.

At the age of three, 99 per cent of girls' speech is comprehensible. It takes boys on the average a year longer. At preschool, about age four, little boys explore things, play vigorously with toy vehicles, build high structures with blocks and then crash them down, and do not care to know the names of their playmates. On the other hand, little girls like to talk and listen, build low structures with their blocks, and welcome strangers (who's names they learn) into their group. Boys make up stories with action and sound effects; girls' stories focus on home, friendship, and emotions. Girls like to take turns in the game of hopscotch; boys prefer the competition of tag. While girls tend to co-operate, share, and act affectionately; boys often engage in conflict, aggression, and destruction of those things they cannot take. [9]

It does not require a rocket scientist to research the facts that men and women begin life being different and they remain that way throughout. The book, *Brain Sex*, was not written by scientists, but it is the compilation of over 400 scientific studies by research scientists in genetics, neurology, psychiatry, biochemistry, endocrinology, and education concerning all aspects of male/female differences. If you need further substantiation for the things written herein, please refer to that book to see a listing of those individual reports.

Yes, men and women are created by God to be distinctly different. This enables each of us to fulfill our roles successfully – for God, for each other, and for ourselves. How a man, who desires to live according to God's Will, discovers and then lives out his role will be the underlying themes of the next four chapters. The importance of what we have just seen about the thinking and personality traits of men and women will become more clear.

NOTES

1. MOIR, ANNE Ph. D. and JESSEL, DAVID, *Brain Sex*, (1992), pp 21-25.

2. STOSSEL, JOHN, ABC news documentary, 2/1/95, *Boys and Girls are Different: Men, Women and the Sex Difference*

3. KIMURA, D., "Understanding The Human Brain" , (1996) *Children's Britannica, Encyclopedia Britannica*, Inc. 136-141.

4. MOIR, ANNE Ph. D. and JESSEL, DAVID, *Brain Sex*, (1992), p. 40

5. KIMURA, D., "Sex, sexual orientation and sex hormones influence human cognitive function," (1996) *Current Opinion in Neurobiology*, 6, 259-263.

6. KIMURA, D. Ibid.

7. MOIR, ANNE Ph. D. and JESSEL, DAVID, *Brain Sex*, (1992), pp 42-49.

8. WEISS, DAVID, "Boys and girls are different," *Kid Currents,* Spring (1998) Vol. 10. No.1 (See also "What Kids Buy and Why: The Psychology of Marketing to Kids," Dan S. Acuff (1997) *New York : Free Press*).

9. MOIR, ANNE Ph.D. and JESSEL, DAVID, *Brain Sex*, (1992), pp 55-64.

SECTION THREE

THE FUNCTIONS OF A BIBLICAL MAN – WHO SHOULD I BE?

An Explanation of Man's Biblical Role

1Timothy 5:8 *But if any provide not for his own, and specially for those of his own house, he hath denied the faith, and is worse than an infidel.*

CHAPTER NINE

PROVIDER

Our study is progressing from, "Who am I?" to, "Who should I be?" God's Word expresses that a Biblical man is expected to function in four key areas of life: as protector, provider, and leader of his family; and cherisher of his wife. These are a part of man's calling (purpose). This and the next several chapters of the book will address each of these four areas in detail.

1Corinthians 7:32b, 33 *He that is unmarried careth for the things that belong to the Lord, how he may please the Lord: he that is married careth for the things that are of the world, how he may please his wife.*

The above verse states that a married man is dedicated to caring (being anxious, seeking to promote one's interests, providing) for worldly things so that he can please his wife.

If any of man's functions is a natural attribute, I believe it would be to provide for his own. There is a natural pride in being the meat-gatherer (the breadwinner) that makes men feel important. No man feels like a whole man if his family's food and necessities come from the government, the church, or any other charity. Depending on others, even for a short period of time, can weaken a man's pride of responsibility and develop a welfare-mentality in his family (the attitude that they deserve being taken care of by others). But, whether it is natural for a man to want to provide for his wife or not, he was assigned the task of being the physical provider as part of his curse for following her leadership into sin:

Genesis 3:17-19 *And unto Adam he said, Because thou hast hearkened unto the voice of thy wife, and hast eaten of the tree, of which I commanded thee, saying, Thou shalt not eat of it: cursed is the ground for thy sake; in sorrow shalt thou eat of it all the days of thy life; Thorns also and thistles shall it bring forth to thee; and thou shalt eat the herb of the field; In the sweat of thy face shalt thou eat bread, till thou return unto the ground; for out of it wast thou taken: for dust thou art, and unto dust shalt thou return.*

To provide for ones self is a normal sign of independence. Young men who stay at home too late in life, slaves, prisoners, welfare recipients, labor union members, tenured professors, and civil service employees – all who come to believe they have a "right" to a job or being taken care of – often lose their desire for independence. On the other hand, the willingness to provide for the needs of a wife and children is one evidence of maturity –the acceptance of responsibility for others at the sacrifice of self.

Physical work, overcoming whatever obstacles are in ones way, and having "a tough road to hoe" is a curse only to the lazy man. Most men feel fulfilled at having overcome the elements by the end of the day. They work out their natural aggression as they compete with themselves or other men. Men who accept God's curse with humility soon find work turns into blessing. The sense of satisfaction that comes from making something with your hands, harvesting a crop, managing a crew of workers, or even in writing a good book cannot be obtained in any other way. Being a good provider should not be a source of sinful pride. The Biblical man sees himself as a conduit of God's provision (grace) through his efforts (submission to the curse of work).

For six thousand years of recorded history men have generally accepted the role of being the provider for their wives and families. In Old Testament times, a widow was to be provided for either by her family or by the nation's tithes. In New Testament times, a widow was to remarry if young; otherwise the church was to provide for her if she had no family. It was considered an act of hedonism for a Christian man not to provide for his own widowed mother, grandmother, or family (1Timothy 5:4-8). The Greek word translated here "provide" means "to consider others needs in advance." Never in Scripture is a woman told to provide for herself or her family. Even as recently as the1950's most civilized men (Christian or not) believed it was their responsibility alone to provide for their wives and families. In fact, any male who refused to work and instead lived off of a woman's income was considered a user, and not a real man.

Unfortunately, men today do not fully sense the honor and advantage of being the sole provider for their families. They say, "What difference does it make if a wife contributes to the family income?" When the wife works outside of the home, it causes her to develop a life apart from her God-ordained purpose – helpmate to her husband and mother to her children. Instead of being able to function fully in support of her husband, she will often become more loyal to her job – or worse yet, her supervisor. The only thing she can provide is money, and that will soon be spent paying for the extra expenses incurred due to her being employed. Any leftover dollars will be spent raising the families' standard of living to a point where she will become a slave to the curse that belongs to man as well as to her own. (Please see the article reproduced at the end of this chapter for a rather complete study on the issue of a wife, especially a mother, working outside of the home. Also see *On the Other Side of the Garden*, chapter eighteen.)

To the extent that a man's wife provides for the family, his role as provider has decreased. (There are situations where a wife's working is possibly necessary: like when there are no children at home and the husband is advancing his education, or when the husband is disabled. *However*, the husband will eventually feel less than a man, and the wife will feel more than a helpmate in these situations.) When a wife contributes financially to the marriage it becomes more of a secular, business partnership than a balanced, Biblical structure. She will have a natural desire to control the family budget, make major purchases, and plan the man's daily expenditures. As a result the other important functions of the man's role can be negatively affected, particularly his leadership. If the wife becomes the major breadwinner, it should not be any surprise that there will likely be increasing pressure from her for a total role reversal. To the extent a wife controls or contributes to the family's finances, she is forced to participate in the family's leadership. A man is better off to face the task of total provision for his family, even if the family could theoretically live at a higher level with both working.

The Biblical man must also provide for his family spiritually:

Genesis 18:19 *For I know him, that he will command his children and his household after him, and they shall keep the way of the LORD, to do justice and judgment; that the LORD may bring upon Abraham that which he hath spoken of him.* (Notice that Sarah was not the one held accountable)

Ephesians 6:4 *And, ye fathers, provoke not your children to wrath: but bring them up in the nurture and admonition of the Lord.*

One of the most destructive results of American men's defection from leading their homes was that women had to assume spiritual leadership for the children. This means that little boys' Bible studies and their understanding of God were influenced by a woman's characteristics of love, forgiveness, and compassion – all from an emotional viewpoint. The problem is not that women cannot teach; it is that they can teach so well! But boys in particular need also to learn about God's justice, righteous, power, and grace. Boys need to learn that Christianity is not just a woman's religion. I believe the move away from teaching about the existence of a literal Hell and eternal punishment for anyone who does not accept Christ as their personal savior, stems from men not teaching in the home and church. Fathers/husbands must lead the family in the worship of God. They must instruct them from the Bible. They must also talk to their children about the character, works, and plan of God in every possible situation. Girls also need to be taught by their daddies to see how important God is to him and the man's perspective on the Word. All children should come to know the integrity (the undivided wholeness) of God's character. He is not only love, He is justice; He is not only righteous, He is grace. Will you teach your children about God?

Deuteronomy 6:7 *And thou shalt teach them diligently unto thy children, and shalt talk of them when thou sittest in thine house, and when thou walkest by the way, and when thou liest down, and when thou risest up.*

Twenty years ago a Christian financial consultant, John Patrick, wrote an insightful article on wives working outside of the home. He operated Personal Management Services in Denver, Colorado at that time, but cannot be located now. His article is printed here for you to consider concerning your wife working. You do not need to have your wife resign her job tomorrow and the family begin starving. Hopefully, at least unmarried young men and women will consider these things before they are trapped.

1. Improper perspective of ownership: With both a husband and wife working, they often develop the idea of 'his' and 'hers' regarding both money and property. This is damaging, divisive, and most serious; a complete distortion of God's design since all that we are and have belongs to God and the husband (as head of the family) is responsible and accountable to God for all of it (no matter what the human source of earnings or the name on the title of the property). Consider: Romans 14:12, 1 Corinthians 6:19-20, 2 Corinthians 5:10, Ephesians 5:21-26, James 1:17.

2. Unfaithful management: If a family "can't make it" on the income God is providing through the head of the family, the need is for faithful management, NOT additional income from a mother working outside the home. God can enable a family to live comfortably on a fhusband's salary if the money is managed according to God's will, but no amount of money will be 'enough' if unfaithfully managed. Consider: Matthew 25:26-30, Luke 16:10-11, Philippians 4:19.

3. Discontentment: The desire to earn money in addition to what God is providing through the head of the family may be evidence of a lack of contentment. We are commanded by God to gratefully accept and to be content (in Him) with what we have. Consider: Matthew 6:28-34, Luke 3:14, Philippians 4:6-7, Philippians 4:11-13, I Timothy 6:8-9, Hebrews 13:5.

4. Conflict of responsibility: The responsibilities of work outside the home may conflict with and draw a mother's time, energy, and devotion away from her family responsibilities. The wife's income may free the husband from the needed pressure and responsibility God has given him to provide for his family. God designed the man to work outside the home, not the woman. Consider: Genesis 3:16-19, Proverbs 14:1, Proverbs 31:10-3, I Timothy 5:8, I Timothy 5:16.

5. Economic loss: A mother working outside the home can actually result in an economic loss In the long run. This is due to many factors that can diminish the 'extra' income such as: increased income taxes, double Social Security payments, child care, extra clothing, transportation, food (extra meals out and convenience foods), housekeeping expenses, and those extra 'you've earned it' expenses. Consider: Ecclisastes 3:1-8, Matthew 25:26-30, Ephesians 5:16-17.

6. Destruction of marriage relationship: The incidence of divorce is much greater where the mother has been working outside of the home. When a mother works outside the home, it may: a) put her in competition with her husband, b) keep her from honoring her husband In the home, c)encourage her to rebel against, rather than submit to, her husband; all because of the independence in terms of time and money that can go with her working. Consider: Genesis 2:18, Genesis 3:16-19, Ephesians 5:21-26, 1Timothy 5:8, I Peter 3:1-4.

7. Failure to fulfill parental responsibilities: Children may be robbed of the love, guidance, and correction needed directly from their mother. Worse, ungodly Influences may be unleashed if the children are not cared for in an atmosphere where Christ is honored as Lord. Consider: Deuteronomy 6:6-9, 1 Samuel 3:13, 2 Chronicles 17:3, Proverbs 13:24, Proverbs19:18, Proverbs 22:6, Proverbs 29:15, 2 Timothy 1:5.

8. Hindrance of testimony to world: Because money Is what the world worships, people of the world (that is, non-believers) are watching how Christians handle financial matters. if any of the problems exist that are described here, it can ruin a Christian family's witness of the life, love, and provision of Christ to them. Consider: John 12:32, Philippians 4:11-13, Philippians 4:19.

1 Peter 3:7 *in like manner, ye husbands, dwell with them according to knowledge, giving honour unto the wife as unto the weaker vessel,*

1 Timothy 2:14 *And Adam was not deceived, but the woman being deceived was in the transgression.*

CHAPTER TEN

PROTECTOR

At one time in America, men would lay down their lives – not just for their wives, but for any woman in danger. When it came to protecting their families in a crisis, like the sinking of the Titanic or fighting in a war, men would make the ultimate sacrifice. For example:

The Titanic, 15 April 1912

> There was an unwritten code of the sea which said "women and children first." It is the natural code that a man operating by Biblical standards will always follow. Several times during the lifeboat loading, the Captain or another officer would shout out the order "Women and children first!" A few men even had to be pulled out of the lifeboats. Nevertheless, with only a few exceptions, most of the Titanic's men willingly gave all of the too-few lifeboat seats to women and children. While the newly-launched Titanic symbolized elegance, invincibility, and man's arrogance; it would now be forever a symbol of duty, chivalry, and faith. A large number of male passengers were Christians and

those men knew well the passage, *Greater love hath no man than this, that a man lay down his life for his friends* (John 15:13). Knowing they had a place reserved in Heaven, they had no need to grasp onto their physical lives. Because of their sacrifice, approximately 75% of the women were saved while only 20% of the men survived.[1]

This was a generation of men of which Great Britain and America could be proud. Their example of chivalry was so outstanding, feminist/suffragettes of 1912 actually argued that the Titanic women were wrong to have accepted seats on the lifeboats from the men. To them the philosophy of men being protectors and defenders of women was offensive and an obstacle to their cause– and it is still.

Do you think men today would make the same sacrifices? Well of course some would. Those men who had been trained in the proper respect of womanhood by their fathers and who had seen it demonstrated in their fathers' lives might. But the average man brought up in the last few generations would be much more likely to think only of saving number one. I am reminded of several startling examples that illustrate this point:

In 1987 a ferry sank in the Philippines killing over 4000 people — *mostly women and children*. The majority of the survivors this time were men. Similarly, when the ferry, Estonia sank in the Baltic Sea, most of its survivors were also men. When the male survivors were questioned why they had not helped the women and children, they were quoted as saying: "Hey, its survival of the fittest," "It was every man for himself," "If women want equality so much — they've got it!" [2]

From the 1970's on, there have been many shocking incidences of modern-day men not coming to the rescue of a woman in distress of which you are probably familiar. For instance, there was the woman who was repeatedly stabbed outside her brown stone apartment door while her terrified neighbors looked on as the killer left and returned multiple times.

Is our attitude about protecting women any more courageous or sacrificial today? It was not in 1992 when a survey was taken among 200 adults called the "Titanic Test." [3] It revealed that:

• If the Titanic sank today, only 67% of the men and 41% of the women would be willing to give up their seat *for their spouses.*

• A little more than 33% of the men would give up lifeboat seats to a woman other than their wives.

• Also, only 55% of both men and women would yield a seat for their own mothers.

I am sure that a lot of women seeing this survey did not feel very secure knowing that one out of every three husbands would not give up their lifeboat seat for them. Additionally not very assuring is the fact that these answers were given on dry land. Do you think those men's actual reactions would be more, or less, sacrificial under the pressure of a real test? I am encouraged, and a little surprised, to see how many American men sacrificed their lives in rescue efforts at the World Trade Center after the September 11, 2001 terrorist attack. However, in every day life, women are still largely unprotected.

A lot of factors have influenced America's men away from a natural protectiveness for womankind. I think there has been an organized attack against womankind at least since the early 1950's. I believe there is evidence to show that women's natural attributes and abilities have been ridiculed and attacked to the point that a majority of young girls today reject motherhood and a wife's historical role. This attack has also caused men to have a negative attitude toward women as a whole – their wives and even their daughters – and it has bred the Feminist Movement.

If our nation is to return to a period of greatness, men will have to accept the role of protector over those who are weak and needy. If the family is to again be strong, husbands and fathers will have to exercise their strength and leadership for the protection of their wives and children. In other words, *we will need Biblical men who are willing to sacrifice their lives for their families.*

Man as the Protector Over His Wife

The Lord sets the pattern for protection:

Deuteronomy 31:8 *And the LORD, he it is that doth go before thee; he will be with thee, he will not fail thee, neither forsake thee: fear not, neither be dismayed.*

Psalm 72:4 *He shall judge the poor of the people, he shall save the children of the needy, and shall break in pieces the oppressor.*

Psalm 91:4,5 *He shall cover thee with his feathers, and under his wings shalt thou trust: his truth shall be thy shield and buckler. Thou shalt not be afraid for the terror by night; nor for the arrow that flieth by day;*

The Lord, as the perfect protector, promises He will go before us, be with us, and not forsake us. He also commands us not to be afraid or to worry. What more could your wife and children ask of you than to lead and accompany them through any kind of danger; and never to desert them when times are tough. Women are naturally insecure, particularly during a real or imagined crisis (a physical threat, danger to her future financial security, potential danger to her children). Cruel teasing or public criticism is never warranted and physical abuse is, of course, totally out-of-line. Men must understand that women really are decidedly weaker than they are and that men are commanded by God to protect them in body, soul, and spirit.

1 Peter 3:7 *Likewise, ye husbands, dwell with them according to knowledge, giving honour unto the wife, as unto the weaker vessel, and as being heirs together of the grace of life; that your prayers be not hindered.*

What does "weaker" actually mean? The Greek word translated weaker is *asthenes* (n), which means: without strength, weak, infirm, inefficient, helpless, feeble, sick, deficient. Depending on context, it can refer to physical, soul, or spiritual weakness (bodily infirmity, moral weakness, or spiritual deficiency). Although this word's use in the gospels, Acts, and 1 Corinthians generally refers to "physical" sickness (Matthew 25:39, 25:43, 25:44; Luke 10:9, 13:11,12; John 5:5; Acts 5:15;16, 20.35; 1 Corinthians 11:30, 12:22; 2 Corinthians 10:10; Galatians 4:13), elsewhere it is clearly used to describe soul and spiritual deficiencies. There is nothing in or around the above verse (1Peter 3:7) that indicates physical illness is the issue.

We know by experience that women are physically weaker than men and that we are to treat them cautiously like a physical part of ourselves (Genesis 2:23,24; Ephesians 5:28,29). For instance, a Biblical man will not allow his wife or daughters to lift or carry heavy loads, to strain at opening difficult containers, or to overwork at anything strenuous. He will not endanger them by allowing them to drive by themselves after dark in our extremely dangerous world; or to drive a car with poor brakes or tires; or to take on too many activities for their nature. The man is also responsible to protect all women from personal physical attack and national danger. Men of 20 years old and up are meant to sign up for military service (Numbers 1: 20-46). Yes, America's and most other country's conscription laws are incorrect – especially Israel's requiring even mothers of newborns to be in military service.

What men are not nearly as aware of about women is their natural soul weakness toward deception and need for protection by their men in this area as well. For instance, daughters and wives should be protected by their fathers or husbands from entering into bad agreements (Numbers 30:3-16). Their emotions are always a potential danger to them and they can easily be deceived by evil people playing on their sympathies and their compassion for others. Therefore, dads must always monitor their unmaried daughter's relationships.

Of course, women also possess an active sin nature which lusts for knowledge, control, and pride from which they need help. Passages where our Greek word *asthenes* indicates moral or soul weakness are Romans 6:19; 8:3 (weak in the flesh "humanity"); 1 Corinthians 8:7,10 (weak in conscience); James 5:14 (repeated sin). Spiritual weakness is indicated by the following passages: Romans 4:19; 14:1,2 (in faith); Hebrews 7:28 (sin). God absolutely does not allow a woman to teach or usurp authority over a man partially because she is subject to deception, particularly by Satan.

1 Timothy 2:12-14 *But I suffer not a woman to teach, nor to usurp authority over the man, but to be in silence. For Adam was first formed, then Eve. And Adam was not deceived, but the woman being deceived was in the transgression.*

The Geek word for "suffer" in this text means to allow, permit, or entrust; "teach" means to instruct with leadership authority; "usurp authority" means to assume power for self without any authorization and the use of the infinitive for that word in the Greek indicates it is her *purpose* to take over leadership from men specifically (rather than from both men and women). The Greek word for "was not deceived" (referring to Adam) means just that, but the word referring to the woman translated "being deceived" means to be deceived *thoroughly*. While Adam chose to transgress, Eve was tricked into her disobedience (cp. 2 Corinthians 11:3). Women are susceptible to deception seemingly through their lust for knowledge (Genesis 3:16), their compulsion to teach others (1 Corinthians 14:33-35 ; 1 Timothy 2:12), their desire to have authority over men (1 Timothy 2:12), and their naturally dominant, emotional nature (including the strong desire to nurture others). Even worse, women who expose themselves spiritually to false doctrine outside of the protection of their male leadership, are subject to Satan's influence:

2 Timothy 3:6,7 *For of this sort are they which creep into houses, and lead captive silly women laden with sins, led away with divers lusts, ever learning, and never able to come to the knowledge of the truth.* (See also Genesis 3:16.)

Biblical men need to regain spiritual leadership of the family. They need to search out Bible-believing, Bible-teaching churches which operate by masculine leadership throughout. They need to monitor for solid Biblical accuracy the "Christian" magazines and books, radio and television shows, and audio and videotapes by which their family is influenced. Even women's and teen's Bible classes and retreats need to be scrutinized by the spiritual leader of the home. Biblical men cannot be indifferent to what influences their families, especially their wives. The very reason America has a female-like religion today is because men in the past defected in their role to protect women in spiritual matters.

Even though women are easily deceived, it does not mean they are of no value or less value in God's plan for mankind. Men need to be aware that women are not chattel or slaves, or even too much trouble; they are held in high esteem by God. When He calls women a weaker vessel, the Greek word He uses for vessel is *skeuos*, an object of purpose, like religious temple equipment (dish or jar) – one that always belongs to God (Acts 9:15; Romans 9:23; 2 Timothy 2:21). We should treat all women with the honor and dignity of fellow heirs of the grace of God (1 Peter 3:7). If men would view all women as valued possessions belonging to God, they would not be so likely to mistreat them. NOTE: Some men treat their wives as if she were one of the boys. They verbally banter with her and occasionally make emotionally hurtful statements. (Worst of all, this habit may lead to teasing her in public about her appearance, her housekeeping, or something else personally derogatory.) God expects men to protect women completely: body, soul, and spirit.

Summary

A husband protects his wife when he sacrifices portions or even all of his life for her safety. He is to consider her natural weaknesses, but not treat her like a child by belittling her. Protection includes not neglecting her while she "does her own thing," as if he had no responsibility. It means to have the character to protect her even from herself. Protection does not mean to control her every action, but to communicate any restrictions deemed necessary for her benefit.

Notes

1. *Titanic Tragedy*, www biblical-counsel.org.
Rev. Peter Hammond here quotes extensively from *A Night to Remember*, by Walter Lord.

2. Ibid.

3. *The Arizona Republic*, April 14, 1992, A.P.

Ephesians 5:25,28,29 *Husbands, love your wives, even as Christ also loved the church, and gave himself for it; So ought men to love their wives as their own bodies. He that loveth his wife loveth himself. For no man ever yet hated his own flesh; but nourisheth and cherisheth it, even as the Lord the church:*

CHAPTER ELEVEN

CHERISH YOUR WIFE

I use the archaic, English word *'cherish'* to help convey the special type of nurturing a Biblical man should express to his wife. This word means: "to hold dear; to feel or show affection for; to keep or cultivate with care and affection." Cherish is not a passive word used simply to describe a concept, but rather, it is an active verb used to describe a manner of expressing love. By contrast, people today generally refer to "love" relationships in the following ways:

1. Love that is based on a desire for what we get from the relationship. For example, "I love her because she makes me feel so good;" or "I love ice cream," which actually means, "I love me, so I give me ice cream."

2. Love that is based on common knowledge, experience, or relationship of friends or family ("Our family always sticks together, right or wrong" or, "He is my best friend, we think almost alike").

3. Love that is based on parental qualities, as in, to treasure, care, nourish, or protect one in need, like a baby.

4. Love that is based on sexual passion, the arousing or temporary satisfying of purely physical, sexual desires; and

5. Love that is based on romantic attraction, an almost mystical drawing together of two people based on their emotions. The affair seems idealistic, titillating, fanciful, adventurous, and exciting. It is usually anti-protocol (against the laws of God, tradition, and/or the rules of society). It is impractical, even magical ("How can it be wrong when it feels so right?" or, "I *think* I love you" as the pop songs have said).

In practice, a Biblical marriage can experience a little of each of these human descriptions. However, Biblical love is far beyond any of them.

Biblical Love Defined

In the Greek language of The New Testament, God uses two words for love: *agape* and *philos*. In a superficial sense, these words can be defined respectively as "love for" and "love of." *Philos* love means "rapport based on mutual knowledge, experiences, and long-time relationships – as love between brothers." God does not command a believer to express *philos*-type love; it can only develop naturally within close relationships. A husband and wife can look forward to experiencing this type of love in time within a Biblical marriage. Examples of *philos* are: God the Father's love of the Son (John 5:20); Christ's love of Lazarus (John 11:36); an unbeliever's love of his own life (John 12:25); a believer who follows Christ's commands and learns of Him (John 15:12-16); Christ's love of a believer that results in His rebuking and chastising him for sin to cause his repentance and restore his fellowship (Revelation 3:19).

Agape is not described by any of the popular terms suggested above since it is virtually unknown in normal life today. Acts of heroism, the sacrifice of knowingly and voluntarily giving up something one has a right to have (life, health, money, possessions, or position) characterizes *agape* love. God commands Biblical men to express this type of love toward their wives. (See Scriptures for *agape* below.)

Agape love forms the very core of the Christian experience. Understanding the following attributes of it can help a man to love his wife Biblically. *Agape*-type love:

1. Expresses true concern for the object of its focus (God, your wife, another person, yourself, or things).

2. Willingly sacrifices self for the benefit (not necessarily to fulfill the desire) of the object – like for your wife. Sometimes, *agape* even means withholding what your wife desires because you know it would be harmful to her.

3. Is defined further by the 12 characteristics in 1Corinthians 13:4–8.

4. Is a facet of the fruit of the Holy Spirit (Galatians 5:22, 23).

5. Proves a believer's faith when expressed toward other believers – such as your wife (1John 4:20,21).

6. Is a mental attitude, not a feeling. Emotions are a response – "I cannot live without her." However, *agape* initiates: *For God so loved the world, that he gave his only begotten Son, that whosoever believeth in him should not perish, but have everlasting life* (John 3:16*)*.

7. Is identified by observers of the actions taken on behalf of the object (John 3:16; 14:21; Romans 5:8; 1John 4-11).

8. Is not based on the value or deeds of the object – *But God commendeth his love toward us, in that, while we were yet sinners, Christ died for us* (Romans 5:8, see also verses 6-7).

9. Is not expressed when a man takes over a wife's role and becomes "the mommy" or *her* helpmate – *Neither was the man created for the woman; but the woman for the man* (1Corinthians 11:9). *For the husband is the head of the wife, even as Christ is the head of the church* (Ephesians 5:23a).

Application

How does this complex expression of love relate to Biblical manhood? Exhibiting *agape* love does not come naturally to human beings. For a man to demonstrate this type of love (as God loves), he must be *thinking* the way God does toward his wife – about what he can do or say for her *benefit*. In other words, to consider what she needs to feel secure, loved, and complete. Her need could be spiritual or in your marriage relationship. When you take the trouble to see her life from her point of view, you are beginning to love her Biblically. Next, you can demonstrate your love by giving up something that you have a right to have, in order to give her something she needs. (Of course you are already giving up approximately forty years of your life working in a job you probably do not really like, possibly working for a boss you cannot stand, for forty or more hours per week plus ten or so additional hours of travel time. But, your wife may not easily understand this as a sacrifice – it is just what men do. She does not know that if you were not working for her and the kids you could: live in a cave with two cardboard boxes for your clothes, a battery-powered laptop with surround-sound, and work as needed doing odd jobs.)

So, to express *agape* love you need to make a real sacrifice, like voluntarily *giving up* Sunday afternoon football to take her and the kids to visit her parents (or anywhere else really important to her, but not you.) Or, be willing *to spend* 15-30 minutes alone with your wife regularly just talking to her (that means no television, newspaper, or toys to distract your attention). To a woman, communication forms the very foundation of her relationships. Remember, *agape* is giving for her benefit, not yours. (However, you may find that you enjoy the improved relationship resulting from her response.) Communicating can also be an excellent time for exercising your leadership (that you will learn about in the next section). Keep this in mind: women are responders to male initiation; they become what we make of them. They will reflect the input of their husbands, good or bad, since they honor (glory) in their men (1Corinthians 11: 7).

Agape love – the mental decision to give sacrificially to someone for their benefit – is also *not based on their value or deeds*. You may have already turned your wife into an award-winning shrew through years of poor leadership and lack of Biblical love. You may now be experiencing the results of your past failure to be a Biblical man: *It is better to dwell in the wilderness, than with a contentious and an angry woman* (Proverbs 21:19);

A continual dropping in a very rainy day and a contentious woman are alike (Proverbs 27:15). But, you married her, and you helped to make her what she is today. Therefore, you must accept the consequences of those actions like a man and at least meet your responsibilities as a husband and a father, even if only dutifully at first. Loving her is not just what you say, but what you do. Treat her with grace: unearned, undeserved love (Romans 5:8). It is the husband who is responsible to demonstrate the analogy of Christ and the Church, totally independent of his wife's action (deeds and words) or attitude:

Ephesians 5:25 *Husbands, love your wives, even as Christ also loved the church, and gave himself for it.*

This statement is a command, not a suggestion. It defines our *minimum* marriage responsibility (as submission does for the woman). Beyond duty, you must choose to love her (even while she is unlovely) like Christ loved us by making His ultimate sacrifice when we were sinners and enemies against God. Remember, *agape* love originates in your thinking, not in your feelings. It is an initiation, a decision, not a response:

Proverbs 23:7 *For as he thinketh in his heart, so is he:*

Philippians 1:9 *And this I pray, that your love may abound yet more and more in knowledge and in all judgment.*

You will need God's Spiritual power in order to have any chance of accomplishing this. Providentially, as a facet of the fruit of His Holy Spirit, every believer walking in the Spirit has daily access to this power. If you are really committed to loving your wife as Christ loved the Church, you might want to post all twelve characteristics of *agape* love God gives us in 1Corinthians 13:4-8 in an inconspicuous spot. Your wife will not want to see it (women do not like to be just another entry on a man's plan or schedule). Your decision and initial follow through may start out strictly in obedience to God, but in time you should find your attitude softening toward your wife, and hers toward you.

Galatians 5:13,14 *For, brethren, ye have been called unto liberty; only use not liberty for an occasion to the flesh, but by love serve one another. For all the law is fulfilled in one word, even in this; Thou shalt love thy neighbour as thyself.* (Your wife is your neighbor – serve her ahead of any other person in your life. Of course, serving her includes leaving her to make a living or maybe to protect your country.)

Your wife may test you several times to see if she can really trust you. The more you have shamed, belittled, and disappointed her in the past, the longer it will take to convince her that you are not just using her again. She may have developed some very wrong responses to your lack of correct leadership over the years – judging, nagging, belittling, yelling, or whatever. Do yourself a favor – win over your wife to the glory of God. Remember, women are built to be responders. If you will initiate to her in love, she should, in time, respond in love.

1 John 16:1 *Hereby perceive we the love of God, because he laid down his life for us: and we ought to lay down our lives for the brethren.* (Your wife is also one of the brethren – this responsibility to love our wives is hard to ignore, is it not?)

You must demonstrate you are *man* enough to take any of her wrong behavior without retaliation and then gently lead her into a Christ-like life as she learns Biblical womanhood. (My wife's books – see titles in back of this book – might be great for this purpose since they were written to help women who were married to men who were not even trying to be Biblical men, like you are now willing to do.) Please understand that the treatment of your wife *is* a testimony to the world of your Biblical love and Christian faith.

Colossians 3:19 *Husbands, love your wives, and be not bitter against them.*

John 13:35 *By this shall all men know that ye are my disciples, if ye have love one to another.*

1 John 4:11 *Beloved, if God so loved us, we ought also to love one another.*

1John 4:21 *And this commandment have we from him, That he who loveth God love his brother also.*

There is no guarantee that an estranged wife will accept your belated love offerings. Many damaged souls do not accept Christ's grace gift of salvation either, but He never ceases to make the offer. I do believe that God will bless your efforts to do right, even if your wife chooses to reject your *agape* love. In any event, you must do what is right.

James 4:17 *Therefore to him that knoweth to do good, and doeth it not, to him it is sin.*

But, if she responds to your genuine love, freely given in her best interests, you will have rescued her from much soul pain and suffering. Her defiance and rejection will turn to admiration and gratitude. *And, you will love it!*

The Core of Estrangement

When a couple reaches the point in their marriage where either of them feels they cannot continue, they usually have become self-centered and self-absorbed. They may say: "I demand my rights," "But what about me?" They need an attitude adjustment from the Word. The next several verses may help them to see their sin, if they truly desire to follow Christ:

Philippians 2:21 *For all seek their own, not the things which are Jesus Christ's.*

Colossians 3:1,2 *If ye then be risen with Christ, seek those things which are above, where Christ sitteth on the right hand of God. Set your affection on things above, not on things on the earth.*

John 5:30 *I can of mine own self do nothing: as I hear, I judge: and my judgment is just; because I seek not mine own will, but the will of the Father which hath sent me.*

Philippians 2:3,4 *Let nothing be done through strife or vainglory; but in lowliness of mind let each esteem other better than themselves. Look not every man on his own things, but every man also on the things of others.*

Galatians 5:13,14 *For, brethren, ye have been called unto liberty; only use not liberty for an occasion to the flesh, but by love serve one another. For all the law is fulfilled in one word, even in this; Thou shalt love thy neighbour as thyself.*

Notice the transition of these verses: from self-centeredness, to loving and serving others.

How to Love Your Wife

Women's emotions are extremely fragile. They are a part of that "weaker vessel" we already studied (1Peter 3: 7). Men need to treat their wives tenderly with words, deeds, and touch. And, please teach your sons to respect all women – especially their mothers.

Ephesians 5:28, 29 *So* (in the same manner as Christ loves the Church, verse 25) *ought men to love their wives as their own bodies. He that loveth his wife loveth himself. For no man ever yet hated his own flesh; but nourisheth and cherisheth it, even as the Lord the church:* (Note added by author.)

The Greek word *ektrepho,* here translated 'nourish,' means to provide all of the physical and mental sustenance that a wife needs (including spiritual doctrine, 1Timothy 4:6). During school, boys came to think they were dumb compared to girls. Many men have carried this false concept into adulthood, partly due to the fact that women can indeed talk more, change subjects faster, and remember details we often wish they would forget. Since most men tend to consider themselves mentally inferior to women, they tend to underestimate their wives' need for a man's leadership and spiritual nurturing.

The second Greek word in the above passage is *thalpo.* It is translated here as 'cherish,' and means to impart warmth or comfort, as a nurse does with children (1Thessalonians 2:7). The English dictionary definition for cherish is: to hold dear; to care for tenderly; give affection; treat as valuable. If a man desires to *agape* his wife in a truly Biblical manner, he will need to practice having a mental attitude of nourishing and cherishing her. His actions will follow naturally.

There are many ways you can show your wife love. Your wife accepts your expression of love when you: talk to her about your plans and dreams; talk with her about anything; and do things together (reading the Word of God and praying, walking anyplace where it is just the two of you.)

The following are some practical ways to express love that are masculine and will not hurt you at all. They each deal with what I believe is the woman's strongest need – a sense of security:

1. Security in physical safety. Protect your home with good door locks, peep holes, alarms, and outside lights. Security also means living in a decent neighborhood, to the extent you can afford. If you are impoverished, live where you must and trust in God (Psalm 4:8). If she must be away from home, often and/or far, provide her with an inexpensive cell phone for emergencies. Protect her in her travels with a remote car alarm she can set off when approaching the car; by not allowing her to go to dangerous locations without you – especially at night; by arming her with a Tazer or mace plus pepper spray (and practice once with her, down wind of course). Unless your wife is a trained expert with a pistol, do not expect one to protect her. A loaded shotgun is much better security in the home and terrifying to a criminal in the hands of a quaking woman. Again, take her out and train her how to hold and shoot it, at whom, and when. If your wife or you have been neutralized against the use of firearms (by the deceptive disarmament propaganda in America), enroll her in a self-defense gun course. Explain that any of these provisions are for your loved ones' safety.

2. Security in you – your love, your commitment, your life. Do not joke about your commitment; never make it contingent. Do not even look at other women or exclaim how attractive one looks. Do not be secretive about where you are going or what you doing away from her. (Women think in pictures and have a prolific imagination.) When she observes that you personally read the Word, have a prayer life, and seek God first on all decisions, her confidence in your leading can be extremely high. Never lie. Be a man, a leader, and face whatever conflicts may occur. Keep your word. Her ability to trust in your word will develop trust in your character.

3. Security in your employment and future. A woman who has committed herself to not pursuing a career, to supporting her husband, to raising his children is extremely vulnerable for his provision. Women cannot stand war games (the maybe-if thinking that a man must go through to consider various possibilities). If you mention to her that your considering a transfer out of state, maybe, someday; she is likely to begin immediately imagining all of the details such a move would require. (She pictures the loss of friends and church, the exchange of her 'home' for just a house, the unknown possibilities of the new state and your new position. She may even picture scratches from the move on her only nice pieces of furniture.) But wait, you have not even told her the alternate possibilities – you are only daydreaming and she has already imagined a plethora of obstacles.

A man must consider his wife's sensitivity in this area when contemplating a major move, or even a simple job change. It is better not to dream out loud at the beginning of his frequent war gaming. When he is satisfied that he is really serious about a particular plan of action, he is ready to get his wife's valuable input. Then he needs to discuss it with her – not as a done deal, but as a reasoned possibility. I am not saying that he needs to ask her permission, or even gain her approval, but he cannot just come home one night and say "I quit my job today and I'm going to buy a hotdog wagon."

4. Security in possessions. A woman needs to nest in a house until it becomes a home – a patchwork of color-coordinated furniture, floor coverings, drapes, pictures, etc. A man can sell his house with a stroke of a pen and have two of his brain-dead friends move all of the furniture with a rental truck on the same day. Men need to consider their wives before, during, and after a move to help make her secure with the whole procedure.

5. Security in finances. Men, you *must* handle the finances; your wives may be excellent with figures, but often they cannot emotionally handle financial problems without trying to solve them on their own (like: go out and get a job, borrow from her Dad, nag you, etc.). She can write the checks if you must; but you determine who to pay, when, and how much. To handle the finances means you *never* allow creditors to harass your wife, you *never* jeopardize the utilities being turned off, and *you* make a plan (part-time job, sell something, refinance, etc.) to solve any shortfall, preferably without upsetting her in the planning. Giving her a reasonable household budget will help her control finances in the home and her feeling of security.

Your employment is a kind of financial security for your wife for the present, but she needs to know you have planned for the future as well. A fairly substantial, 20-year "term" life insurance policy for a 30-year-old (say $100,000 per dependant) is not expensive (about $8/ month for $100,000; $25/ month for $500,000). Health insurance is almost a must today and if not provided by your employer, I highly recommend Samaritan Ministries' inexpensive plan for Christian families' major medical coverage.[4] There are some Christians who believe owning any kind of insurance equals not trusting God for your provision. Certainly, they should not violate their own conscience (1Corinthains 8:7). However, we are each responsible not to become a burden on others through the poor handling of our finances or by practicing a reckless lifestyle. I suppose one could show his trust in God by never working and have the family gather around the dinner table to see what God would provide. Or, walk across the street with a blindfold on to prove God will protect. But as Jesus said to Satan, *Thou shalt not tempt the Lord thy God* (Matthew 4:7b). Remember, God sets forth the industrious ant as a positive example (Proverbs 6:6); and working for your food as a requirement of Christian responsibility (2 Thessalonians 3:10).

The three, most important practices you can do to provide financially for the future are: (1) Eliminate any high interest debt no matter what it takes – it is a crisis to your financial health. (2) Do not pay any more taxes than absolutely required (make the maximum contribution allowable *throughout the year* on individual retirement plans – IRA's, KEOGH's, 401K's). This reduces your taxes, sets up a savings plan, and accumulates interest all at once. (Do not withdraw these funds – they are your future!) (3) Buy a home if at all possible – it allows you the only interest deduction left, is likely to appreciate over several years, and is the average man's only protection from runaway inflation. Otherwise, live within your means; if God does not provide the finances, do not insult His provision by taking money from your already-made commitments or squander your future savings. Avoid eating expensive meals out. Do not go shopping without knowing what you *need* to buy and having done your comparisons for the best price beforehand. Do not buy on impulse; nobody has enough money to waste. There is more, but this should give you the basics.[5]

In conclusion, the more secure your wife is, the more she can trust your leadership. When she is convinced that you are in charge, led by God, and have hers and the children's best interests at heart, the easier it will be for her to submit to you and return your love.

Notes

1. *A GREEK-ENGLISH LEXICON of the NEW TESTAMENT*, by William F. Arndt and F. Wilbur Gingrich, Zondervan Publishing House, 1973.

2. *American Heritage Dictionary*, 1996 edition

3. *WorldNet Dictionary*, Princeton University, 1997 edition

4. Samaritan Ministries (www.samaritanministries.org), 1-888/ 268-4377

5. Larry Burkett's Crown Financial Ministries (www.crown.org) P.O. Box 100 Gainesville, GA 30503-0100.

SECTION FOUR

THE ULTIMATE ROLE OF BIBLICAL MANHOOD – LEADERSHIP

Lead, Follow, or Get Out of the Way

This final facet of Biblical Manhood is so extensive it will require several chapters to explain. Leadership is an omni-directional function: husband, father, church, occupation, and even additional ones for some men. It is a particularly difficult subject because men today have had few role models and virtually no instructions on being a leader. In many areas we are so far removed from our Biblical role that it may be a little bit of a shock to see how far we have drifted. But, I believe the following chapters will present information that will be logical, understandable, and with God's help, life changing. Do not be disheartened if you find you fall short of Biblical Manhood, with God *all* things are possible!

Hebrews 2:6b-7 *What is man, that thou art mindful of him? or the son of man, that thou visitest him? Thou madest him a little lower than the angels; thou crownedst him with glory and honour, and didst set him over the works of thy hands:*

Genesis 1:28 *And God blessed them, and God said unto them, Be fruitful, and multiply, and replenish the earth, and subdue it: and have dominion over the fish of the sea, and over the fowl of the air, and over every living thing that moveth upon the earth.*

CHAPTER TWELVE

UNDERSTANDING BIBLICAL LEADERSHIP

Mankind was given an assignment by God: to procreate and subdue all of physical creation;[1] and to rule all living creatures.[2] The woman was created to help the man be successful in these endeavors as his counter-part.

To man alone was delegated the authority (the power and right to rule) in several specific areas of human life: marriage, parenting, government, and church. (Women are delegated authority only in parenting and even that authority is under the leadership of their husbands.) Not every man is called to function in all of these areas at once; but to be successful in any position of authority requires character and leadership ability. This chapter will describe that ability and how it should develop in men.

With all of the positions of leadership required of men (plus business for some), it should be obvious that every man needs to know a great deal more about leadership than most men know today. Without proper parenting or observing other mature men acting as role models, young men grow up not even understanding their purpose, let alone *how* to lead. Common sense (sound, practical judgment that is independent of specialized knowledge) is also a lost attribute today. Since modern young people's thinking comes mostly from being influenced by superficial, celebrity personalities and from their own peers (who are filled with an assumed importance of their own arrogant opinions), they have little exposure to sound judgment. Do not despair. If you were one of these un-parented youth, you can still become a Biblical leader; but you must first face your deficiencies and renew your mind to God's point of view (Romans 12:1,2).

Who Are The Roles Model For Today's Men?

Perhaps you were blessed to have someone of good character who acted as your role model. It could have been your own father, a relative, teacher, pastor, or coach. Thank God for such a gift. But to whom do young men see as role models if they are not so blessed? They could look to big business and definitely find some leaders (for instance: Bill Gates or Donald Trump), but they might learn more about greed and ruthlessness than about godly character from their examples. They could evaluate our government leaders (for instance: Presidents Nixon or Clinton), but then they might learn mostly about lying, dishonesty, arrogance, and lust for power and sex. They might turn to the heroes of the sports world; but then they would see the foul-mouthed, temper-tantrums of a Bobby McEnroe or Dennis Rodman. They could only learn immaturity, immorality, rebelliousness, and self-centeredness from these examples. Certainly, few character traits beneficial to self or others would likely be gleaned from any of these icons.

Maybe our young men could look to the movies for portrayals of manliness. The contrast seen there between the machismo of a Dirty Harry, James Bond, or Arnold Schwarzeneger character might be attractive when compared to effeminate men they know in real-life; but, imbalanced manhood is not what they need to learn. Finally, they could look to leaders in religion (for instance: Jimmy Swaggart, Jim Bakker, and a myriad of Catholic Priests who have sexually or financially betrayed the trust of others). They could learn by these examples that true godliness does not necessarily equate with those who hold positions of being popular religious leaders. The real heroes of the past were modest, quiet men who stood for what was right and were willing to die for that stand. In their place we have males who are openly anti-authority, who use and abuse women, who are immoral in their business dealings, and whose language mimics the lowest levels of society – not the best of role models! Of course, there are exceptions to our lost heroes, such as those who saved students at the school shootings, individual acts of bravery nationwide every year, and the hundreds of firemen, policemen, and others who risked and even lost their lives trying to save victims at the World Trade Center. But, I am referring here to role models whose lives exemplify Biblical leadership day in and day out in everything they do.

Elements of Biblical Leadership

There are at least three essential elements that make up Biblical leadership. They are: a Biblical perspective, a godly character, and a healthy ego. Let us take a non-exhaustive look at each of these elements.

Biblical perspective – the book you are reading is intended to direct you on a path to reach this objective. Most men will need to re-read at least some chapters several times to assimilate the information, since it may have been foreign to their thinking before now. You will also benefit by studying the lives of Abraham, Joseph, Moses, David, Daniel, Paul and others in the Bible. These men portray many of the correct characteristics of Biblical Manhood. Even though most of them made mistakes or sinned, you will gain greatly by studying these men's failures and how they dealt with them.

Godly character – study the above histories for these examples:

1. **Commitment** to God and legitimate responsibility (even under personal sacrifice, ridicule, persecution, and on-going hardship);

2. **Self-discipline** ("When the going gets tough, the tough get going" kind of attitude). Doing what is right, even when it is disagreeable to you, develops self-discipline;

3. **Self-confidence** through total dependence on God (the personal independence strived for today is merely the modern expression of Cain's arrogance – "I want to do it my way");

4. **Personal accountability** for one's own actions (facing responsibility without hiding behind self-justification, blaming others, or life's multiple circumstances);

• Openly admitting your fault to those you have wronged.

• Confessing to God.

• Making full restitution to man – paying for what your error, accident, or sin cost others.

• And, accepting the legitimate consequences for your actions – loss of privilege, loss of employment, even loss of life.

Quality of leadership originates from the quality of a man's own character.

Most of today's untrained men are not well qualified in the above leadership traits. This is demonstrated by their reluctance to make a permanent commitment to a wife. Even when they do, they continue being insecure in their knowledge, skill, or experience to lead "through thick and thin."

Leadership requires commitment to a purpose beyond mere self-protection. It takes self-discipline to pay the cost to make things right. Today's men generally lack the character of Biblical manhood to make decisions and then stand accountable for the results – good or bad. They do not realize that not deciding at all can often be worse than making a wrong decision, which can at least be learned from and possibly rectified.

Some men fear a marriage commitment due to their lack of self-confidence (they cannot satisfy themselves that they possess all of the facts about such an important decision, i.e. they think they might make a mistake). One can never gather all of the facts before hand; or know what will happen in the future. If we did have all-seeing and all-knowing ability, we might then believe we did not need to depend on God. Consider the following situation that only God could have foreseen:

A man marries an intelligent, vibrant girl who later becomes crippled, or seriously ill. The proof of Biblical manhood is not in having avoided this marriage, buying more health insurance, or using this tragedy as an excuse for a marital affair; it is in the character to deal rightly with the tragedy. A man in this situation could exhibit commitment, self-discipline, self-confidence, and accountability – Biblical maturity. He also can demonstrate agape-love as he willingly lays down his life for another.

It is no wonder that so many of today's immature, single males cannot leave home. Never having been trained to be a mature man, they remain in, or return to, the nest and to a life of irresponsibility. Or, they may instead form immoral partnerships with independent, also untrained women, thereby missing the plan of God for each of them. Such immature, young males likely possess badly damaged egos.

The Male Ego

The word ego comes from the Greek word that means "I" in the emphatic sense as in "I, and I only." The Lord told Moses that He should be identified as being "I AM that I AM" in Exodus 3:14. Ego emphasizes the uniqueness of the individual. It is not a good or a bad thing in itself; it is also not equivalent to pride. Pride is one of the worst of sins on God's list (Proverbs 6:16, 8:13). It is Biblically defined as thinking too highly *or* too lowly of yourself, i.e. giving yourself too much credit (I am the greatest) or too little (aw shucks, tell me again how good I am).

The dictionary definition of ego is: "the I or self of any person; a person as thinking, feeling, and willing; and, a person distinguishing himself or herself from the selves of others and from objects."[3] Ego is also defined as the way one views himself in relationship to what he thinks his role is. Simply put, it is one's unique identity. Ego can be expressed positively as a correct evaluation of oneself or negatively as egotism, but its purest meaning is simply the recognition of self as distinct from others. When a man's ego is healthy, it is manifested by his self-confidence, courage, and decisiveness. These traits help enable a man to be the leader of his family. Ego initially expresses itself when boys are young. It is what happens then and afterward that makes a difference whether it will be healthy or damaged.

Even at an early age, boys often feel protective toward their mothers. They will respond quite seriously to the idea of being the 'man of the house' while Daddy is away. Leading and protecting women correspond to their masculine egos and makes them feel valuable, needed, and right about themselves. Anyone who has watched young boys at play has observed their untrained egos. Most boys begin very early in life wanting to be a winner and are willing to do almost anything to beat others. They compete in everything, including arguing over whose dad can whip anyone else's dad.

Each boy's confidence is undaunted. He is positive he will be the one to win the next game (even though he has lost ten in a row), or that he will be the first to rocket to Mars. This driving force later supports the courage to protect and provide for his family, as well as the confidence to lead. The instinctive desire to excel is a good and natural part of a boy's developing manliness, but the tactics for achieving this objective can be distorted by his untrained and unrestrained nature to sin. It can, therefore, produce immature egotism.

It is God's design for parents to restrain their sons' sin natures and train them to express their natural drive to excel in acceptable ways. However, lack of proper child training has distorted the egos in the majority of today's men. As a result, many men exhibit egotism (exaggerated self-importance, sinful pride, and cruelty). Even a larger number of men have had their egos damaged severely enough to produce insecurity, indecisiveness, passivity, and cowardliness in them. Either type of distortion will result in a man's inability to lead his wife and family properly.

In past generations, twelve-or thirteen-year-old boys eagerly took on newspaper routes. They not only carried and threw the heavy papers in all kinds of weather, they had to collect the customers' money. If they made any mistakes in delivering or collecting, they suffered the consequences. This type of training – handling a paper route, working on a farm, or working in the family business – has helped many young men to grow up. In recent generations, however, I have actually seen mothers (not even dads) helping their little boy with his paper route in inclement weather. Do these mothers (and their non-leader husbands) not know that they could not do any more damage to their son's manhood if they used a knife and made him into an eunuch? Parents diminish their son's masculinity by treating him like a girl, by fostering his fear of pain (from athletics, relationships, embarrassment, etc.), and by not letting him experience the consequences of his own failures.

Manliness is an important component of a man's ego. It is a man's viewpoint of himself that gives him the confidence, objectivity, and initiative to be a leader. Proper manliness initiates leadership. It initiates a desire to protect and provide – two of the ways a well-balanced man expresses his love for his wife and children. The male ego and masculinity are so closely intertwined that if the ego is damaged, the manliness will be as well. If you are one of those thousands of today's men who suffered a damaged ego in childhood and lack proper manliness, I suggest that you seek to become spiritually mature by gaining a thorough knowledge of Scripture without delay. Also, read some of the following real-life biographies of masculine heroes you may have missed while growing up: Booker T. Washington, Theodore Roosevelt, Martin Luther, Pastor Wurmbrand, Winston Churchill, Patrick Henry, Robert E. Lee, etc.

The following chart may help you envision the extremes of man's ego, where you now stand, and how far you must develop. Understand that your development as a Biblical leader will require time for you to:

Learn – the Word of God;
Trust – in His Word, and;
Depend – on God's power.

This transformation of your thinking is not like the superficial decision of a child wishing to go to Mars – this is real-life manhood!

Ego

EXPRESSIONS OF A PROPERLY DEVELOPED MASCULINE EGO
(The male ego should be developed into maturity to prepare a young man for his roles of leadership and conquering the physical universe.)

> Leadership Drive
> Confident
> Acceptance of Responsibility
> Courageous
> Personal Accountability
> Objective Oriented
> Desire to Succeed
> Protective

EXPRESSIONS OF A DISTORTED OR DAMAGED SELF-IMAGE
(The normal male ego can be distorted by the human nature of sin, poor child training, or by a belittling parent or wife.)

> Superiority
> Inflated Ego
> Self-Centered
> Aggressive
> Arrogant
> Combative

OR   Inferiority
> Passive
> Insecure
> Cowardly
> Selfish

Figure 12.1   Mature and distorted male egos

May God encourage you and bless you as you: *press toward the mark for the prize of the high calling of God in Christ Jesus* (Philippians 3:14).

Notes

1. Subdue: Hebrew, *kabash*, "to subdue, bring into bondage, tread down with the feet; thus to dominate." (Zechariah 9:15; Micah 7:19; Jeremiah 34:11,16; 2 Chronicles 28:10; Nehemiah 5:5). In Genesis 1:28, God commanded man to control the natural resources and intended for man to study, conquer, and use every aspect of the environment wisely or foolishly as he chose. (Examples of proper science: space travel, organ transplants, hydroponics, etc.) The pagans have instead always worshiped creation, used up the natural resources, and seldom cultivated anything.

2. Rule: Hebrew, *radah*, "have dominion, rule, dominate" over someone or something." Used here to indicate a position of dominance. Like subdue above, rule is a command in Genesis 1:28. Man (under God) was created to rule, have dominance over, all living creatures (except other human beings).

3. *American Heritage Dictionary*, 1996 edition; 1: the self especially as contrasted with another self or the world; 2 a: Egotism; b; Self-esteem and *Merrian-Collegate Dictionary*, 2002 (caution: all modern dictionaries contain an abundance of psychology's unsubstantiated opinions as to what ego means. These must be carefully evaluated before accepting.)

Genesis 18:19 *For I know him, that he will command his children and his household after him, and they shall keep the way of the LORD, to do justice and judgment;*

CHAPTER THIRTEEN

CHRISTIAN CHARACTERISTICS OF LEADERSHIP

In twenty-five years serving as Vice-President of Accelerated Christian Education, CEO and Chairman of the Board of Alpha Omega Publications, and operating smaller businesses, I have been exposed to several descriptions of a leader. Great teachers on management such as Peter Drucker, Ted Engstrom, William Onchen, and others have attempted to capture the essence of leadership character. The following principles draw on what I remember of their writings plus a recent speech by Norman R. Augustine, former Chairman of Martin Marietta. He said, "Leadership cannot be taught: but it can be learned. Leadership emerges out of experience – from falling and learning and trying again." [1] (This procedure may be what it takes to develop that "no-fear" attitude we hear so much about today.)

It is difficult to prioritize the following qualities; each one is important, if not essential. My recommendation would be for you to make a priority of each quality in which you are weakest and commit yourself to becoming victorious in those areas first. This approach should provide you with the most-dramatic personal improvement.

Characteristics of a Leader

Authority. Here is a word all rebels hate. Sadly, we live in a society where most adults have been reared to feel that they should always get their own way. For a thorough presentation on authority, please study the chapter, "Principles of Authority," in my book, *What the Bible Says About...Child Training, 2nd Edition* (pp.31-36). [2]

There have been a number of attacks against Biblical authority by professing Christian writers in recent years. These writers reject God's teaching on the subject and set forth apostasies from psychology and/or new-age philosophy as substitutes. The best way to spot a counterfeit is to know the real thing. Only when you know what the Bible teaches about parents' proper use of corporal punishment, about a husband's authority in marriage, or about a leader's responsibility to decide the direction for those under him to follow, can you recognize and discard the false.

Vision. God's Word says, *Where there is no vision, the people perish* (Proverbs 29:18): Vision is simply seeing the unseen; seeing what needs to be done or where to go; i.e., a plan. Followers need to have leaders who direct their activities. Without long-range vision, we will each allow our work 'to expand to fill the time allotted.' Although subordinates can offer suggestions, the leader is the only one in a position to envision all of the factors involved. He then must make the lonely decisions (neither leadership nor accountability can be shared) that bring about an intelligent charge toward the objective.

The concept of vision is difficult to explain in today's society since most decisions are made 'on the fly,' 'by the seat of the pants,' 'off the top of the head.' These sayings indicate that we often do not use research, evaluation of data, or mental analysis in our decision-making. If this is our approach, we cannot look ahead intelligently; we can only react or respond to problems and opportunities on the basis of our emotions at the moment. Without vision initiative is impossible; and so is leadership. A man without initiative just allows life to happen to him. Proper vision could be demonstrated by a homeschool father who annually evaluates the progress of each of his children; and then carefully maps out a comprehensive program for their further education. (If you have dumped parenting and educational responsibilities totally on your wife's back, you are not providing the leadership your family needs.)

Vision is when a business owner lays out a plan to reach specific objectives and then carefully communicates that plan to his subordinates (including all modifications as the plan progresses). Without good communication, visions turn into frustrated dreams. Vision is expressed in the home when a father charts all of the household duties to be done on a regular basis and assigns them to specific children. He helps Mom realize that these are a vital part of child training, even if the children do a poor job during their learning curve. He then faithfully follows up on the children daily while Mom trains them to be proficient in each task, eventually decreasing her workload.

Our Lord is the example of a leader with a vision:

Hebrews 12:2 *Looking unto Jesus the author and finisher of our faith; who for the joy that was set before him endured the cross,*

Competence. The past several generations have spawned more incompetent workers than all of history, in my biased opinion. It seems that many people expect to be paid simply because they show up (or even when they do not). We need a generation of men who will become competent in their respective fields. These men then need to teach their boys the pride of workmanship that being competent brings. God's Word again has helpful instructions for us:

1. Building your plan on a solid foundation.

Matthew 7: 24-27 *Therefore whosoever heareth these sayings of mine, and doeth them, I will liken him unto a wise man, which built his house upon a rock: And the rain descended, and the floods came, and the winds blew, and beat upon that house; and it fell not: for it was founded upon a rock. And every one that heareth these sayings of mine, and doeth them not, shall be likened unto a foolish man, which built his house upon the sand: And the rain descended, and the floods came, and the wind blew, and beat upon that house; and it fell: and great was the fall of it.*

Competence in leadership means to know what you are doing, what resources to use, the suitability of the location, the estimated time to complete, and who is needed. It also means to seek out wisdom from those who have experience about the project. Some men in positions of leadership have convinced themselves that proper planning is not necessary (waste of time, problems will still develop, etc.). They enjoy problem solving and getting out of tight spots. However, most problems in projects originate from lack of planning.

2. Count the costs.

Luke 14: 28-30 *For which of you, intending to build a tower, sitteth not down first, and counteth the cost, whether he have sufficient to finish it? Lest haply, after he hath laid the foundation, and is not able to finish it, all that behold it begin to mock him, Saying, This man began to build, and was not able to finish.*

Finding that the cost is too high for a project envisioned does not mean it must be abandoned, just reevaluated and a different approach taken. A good leader takes carefully evaluated risks, but he is not a gambler.

3. Consider the obstacles that could make the project fail.

Luke 14: 31-32 *Or what king, going to make war against another king, sitteth not down first, and consulteth whether he be able with ten thousand to meet him that cometh against him with twenty thousand? Or else, while the other is yet a great way off, he sendeth an ambassage, and desireth conditions of peace.*

A positive attitude or sizable ego (which most natural leaders possess) is not enough to overcome every obstacle. Even if they can beat the odds, the cost may exceed the benefit. There is no value in winning the battle just to lose the war. However, many obstacles can be prevented or conquered with proper planning.

Character. Leadership exposes the integrity (wholeness) of your soul. You may fool your friends and neighbors, but your wife knows the real you. Your direct subordinates in management also learn a lot about you and your deficiencies. Character starts with what you think, *For as he thinketh in his heart, so is he* (Proverbs 23:7). Let us explore some godly character traits:

> **1. Honesty** is the top attribute on my list; if people cannot trust your words they will not follow you for long. God's Word gives a less-than-flattering statement on man's honesty, *God is not a man, that he should lie; neither the son of man, that he should repent: hath he said, and shall he not do it? or hath he spoken, and shall he not make it good?* (Numbers 23:19). Where would you be in your relationship with God if you could not implicitly trust His Word? Ones entire character is judged by his honesty. (Note: dishonesty as a sin against God is not being dealt with here.)
>
> The Biblical man needs to become godlike in his honesty to others. He should not lie or fail to make good on a previous commitment. The only way a man can train himself to keep his word is consistently to pay the consequences of his insufficiently-considered promises and even those plans that are truly sabotaged. Like any other wrong we do to another person, dishonesty must be *acknowledged* (admitted as a wrong to those hurt), *repented* of (saying and then changing direction so as not to repeat the action), and *made restitution* to those hurt (pay *all* of the cost, plus some – the Biblical example would indicate at least double).

When a man gives his word it must be a one-sided covenant (contract); not just his best intentions if nothing happens to get in the way. If a man's word can be relied on only if nothing else interrupts him, it is no commitment. (Remember the times you have told your children you would X with them on Saturday and then casually broken your word? How about the many times you have promised your wife to fix Y in the house and then allowed a new problem at work, another person, or your own wants to prevent you from following through – for weeks.) Is it any wonder that your trusting wife, who once believed your every word, now sighs or looks out of the tops of her eyes when you throw out another of your worthless promises? Could this explain why your young-adult children, who once naively believed you could pull off and hide one of your fingers, now ignore almost any words you say?

Some men have a habit of giving 'cheap promises.' These are semi-intentions given (usually under pressure of subordinates) to put off making a decision, to stop the pressure temporarily, to make oneself appear to be cooperative or giving, or etc. We probably learned this trick to avoid responsibility in childhood. We found that our parent(s) would easily accept a promise in place of obedience and seldom followed up. Many men have continued this deception to their detriment.

Recommendation: NEVER give your word to anyone unless you are willing to keep it *or pay the consequences*. If you absolutely must break your word to your children, double the X they were going to receive – and make it soon! If you absolutely cannot fix the Y for your wife, hire Mr. fix-it or buy a new one out of your own money (better yet, fix Y that night or the next morning before doing anything else). Repeated excuses for failure and apologizes for unfulfilled intentions are worthless. Restoring the damage and changing your character are the only things that will make your word have value with those who have been let down by you. Business illustration: The boss tells his employees that they can quit working at 5 P.M., but he has a habit of coming up with last-minute projects due to his poor planning. He then expects, or demands, his servants to work intensely or overtime to make up for his oversights. The boss's word, of course, is compromised even though he may repeatedly give excuses or profusely apologize. If he desires to be trusted in the future, he will have to consider the real cost of his projects, allow ample time for them to be done during normal working hours, move them to a later date, or do the project himself. Several times of paying the consequences will make him a better manager and a more honest person. Until a man willingly pays the cost of his broken words, he is not likely to ever become honest. He will even lie to himself in an attempt to justify his lies.

2. Courage is also essential for leadership. When a man is fearful of what people might think or say negatively about his actions, his leadership has been neutralized. Read this brilliant article from a friend of mine:

We don't know what Adam was feeling, but why didn't he stand up to his wife? It would have taken courage to contradict her, to correct her. He may have risked her favor. There seems to be nothing worse for a passive, unconfident man than to have his wife unhappy with him. The easy thing to do was to go along. It was also easier than confronting that wily serpent. We can imagine Adam saying to her, " Yes dear, I'm sure it is a very good piece of fruit. Whatever you say dear." The alluring thing about cowardice is that it seems to make everybody happy. Failing to stand for principle or to correct those who are in the wrong keeps things peaceful. Of course, it may lead the whole human race into millennia of sin and misery, but hey, it keeps the wife happy today! The failure of manly courage has cost the world dearly. Our nation is cursed today with men who are afraid to be leaders at home. For so many men their greatest desire is simply to keep peace within the family at any price. What the wife wants she gets, what the children want they get, unless the demand is so outrageous that Dad has to get angry and then sulk about their forcing him to take a stand. Do you take your stand to lead your family according to principle even when they disagree, or others outside the family don't understand? Are you willing to be unpopular with your charges for the sake of protecting them from evil companions and environments? Is pleasing God more important to you than pleasing men (or women, or children)? One sure mark of a leader is his willingness to take actions that bring him under attack from those who don't share his understanding of what it means to please God. The family leader is a man of courage because he fears God. [3]

3. Self-discipline is extremely important for any leader; it shows that you are in control of yourself, your word, your time, and your priorities. Subordinates must utilize self-discipline to be successful and you are their example (1 Corinthians 9:27). Follow-through and perseverance come from self- discipline.

4. Loyalty inspires others to follow. Your loyalties to God and your superiors are examples to those under your authority. Passion for the goals you are assigned also motivates your followers– like the pep-talk of a coach. And, having the courage of your convictions is also inspiring. Loyalty is not a blind allegiance to a person or a cause; it is *only* deserved by men or causes of Biblical character.

5. Open communication is a key element of leadership. Secretive men make poor leaders. It is unfair for a wife or an employee to have to guess what the leader expects them to do. Leaders must first be willing and then they must become able to communicate. God makes His Will known to man (Genesis 2:16; John 20:31), and

1 John 5:13 *These things have I written unto you that believe on the name of the Son of God; that ye may know that ye have eternal life, and that ye may believe on the name of the Son of God.*

6. Love. This is the agape-type love we examined in Chapter Ten. A leader must have true concern for the benefit of those in his charge. If a husband does not care about his wife's needs, or a pastor about his sheep, or a company president about his employees, they will read his lack of concern and withhold a part of their loyalty, effort, and commitment.

Philippians 2:3 *Let nothing be done through strife or vainglory; but in lowliness of mind let each esteem other better than themselves.*

Romans 13:9b.10 *Thou shalt love thy neighbour as thyself. Love worketh no ill to his neighbour: therefore love is the fulfilling of the law.*

Vision, competence, and *quality character* partially distinguish a leader from the crowd. But, every man is a leader in at least one area of his life. You may be in training for a higher calling right now.

The following article introduces every issue of The Patriarch magazine as it deals with masculine leadership:

A Call to Leadership – Patriarchy

"Men must look back to the past so that they can look to the future with hope. They need to repent of generations of failed leadership. They need to learn to do what great men of the past did: to fear the Lord and delight in his commands. They need to again accept the burden of godly leadership. Only then will the prospects for the future of our nation brighten. Patriarch is a word that captures what it is that men must again become if our society is to be redeemed. Here is what author, Weldon Hardenbrook, has to say about this seldom-used term.

"'Where did the role of fatherhood come from? The essence of fatherhood is best understood in one word that Americans,

even Christian Americans, have totally lost the meaning of, a word against which all the enemies of God have warred in an attempt to secure its annihilation. A word that has been abused, trampled on, ignored, or vehemently spit upon and mocked by raging hyper feminists and discarded by irresponsible, self-centered, hedonistic males. A word so powerfully significant and loaded that the feminized, peace-at-any-price boys religiously relegate it to ancient days of antiquity. A word that has become unmentionable among its owners and exiled to the company of obscene four-letter words in the minds of most male and female Americans. But whether we use this word or not, without its recovery, without its function being made known and its reality working in society, there is absolutely no clear, positive way to redeem the male identity. This word can never be neutral. It was worn by the men of old, from Abraham to David, and it needs to belong to American men today. What is this awesome word that must be understood? This role that must be reclaimed? The word is patriarchy. It is awesome because it is in the meaning of this word that fatherhood exists and the foundation of the male identity is supplied. The biblical term patriarchy is derived from two words in the Greek language, patria (taken from the word pater, father), which means family; and arche, which means beginning, first in origin, and to rule. A patriarch is a family ruler. He is the man in charge." [4]

What is needed today is nothing less that a return to patriarchy, a society led by strong, godly men. We need family leaders who will also become leaders in the churches and throughout every institution in the nation. Such men must also learn to see beyond today, to see themselves as just the beginning of what will be many generations who will be mighty in the land. Each man should aim to be the founder of a dynasty for God." [5]

At least I am not the only one speaking these things! Will you accept this challenge?

Notes

1. "Characteristics of a Leader," a speech by Norman R. Augustine, April 29, 1999; *CSIS News and Events*.

2. *What the Bible Says About...Child Training*, 1980, by J.Richard Fugate, Foundation for Biblical Research.

3. *PATRIARCH* magazine, www. patriarch.com/ article on "Male Passivity" PO Box 50, Willis, VA 24380, Phil Lancaster, Publisher.

4. *Missing from Action: Vanishing Manhood in America* (first edition, pp. 139-140), Weldon Hardenbrook

5. *PATRIARCH* magazine, www. patriarch.com/ "Why Patriarch"? (inside cover) PO Box 50, Willis, VA 24380, Phil Lancaster, Publisher.

1 Corinthians 6:2,3 *Do ye not know that the saints shall judge the world? and if the world shall be judged by you, are ye unworthy to judge the smallest matters? Know ye not that we shall judge angels? how much more things that pertain to this life?*

Revelation 5:10 *And hast made us unto our God, kings and priests: and we shall reign on the earth.*

CHAPTER FOURTEEN

THE MULTIFACETED ROLES OF THE BIBLICAL MAN

Mankind (specifically men) was established by God to be rulers in creation's chain of command. Every man must face the fact that he is a leader and possesses authority from God to enforce his many roles as defined by Him (Romans13:1-4). These roles can include: husband, father, patriarch, civil government, church government, business management, and others. This chapter will discuss the roles that apply most to the family.

Marriage

Genesis 2:18 *And the LORD God said, It is not good that the man should be alone; I will make him an help meet for him.*

1Corinthians 11:8,9 *For the man is not of the woman; but the woman of the man. Neither was the man created for the woman; but the woman for the man.*

Genesis 2:24 *Therefore shall a man leave his father and his mother, and shall cleave unto his wife: and they shall be one flesh.*

Ephesians 5:23a *For the husband is the head of the wife, even as Christ is the head of the church:*

Genesis 3:16b *and thy desire shall be to thy husband, and he shall rule over thee.*

God ordained the responsibility for leadership of the woman to the man from the very beginning (1Corinthians11:3). She was created *from* the man and *for* the man and as a helpmate suitable *for* him. (She was not designed by God to be an equal partner with man or to pursue her own career or direction.) Man was the first-born of creation mankind, and therefore was its ruler (1Timothy 2:13). He was even given the authority to name the woman. In The Fall, man was held responsible for listening to and following his wife's leadership into sin, further making it clear who was accountable (Genesis 3:17-19). After The Fall, man's position of rulership became part of the woman's curse because she had allowed herself to be duped by a tempter; and then usurped man's authority (Genesis 3:16). (See also, 1Timothy 2:14 and 2 Timothy 3:6,7.)

The Mystery of Marriage

Marriage is extremely important to God. It depicts the joining together of His Son Jesus Christ and The Church – the Bride made up of all believers after the Cross. A Biblical mystery (*musterion* in the Greek) does not mean a puzzle that cannot be figured out or a secret that is beyond understanding as it normally means in the English. *Musterion* stands for "the secret thoughts, plans, and dispensations (distribution, order, or era) of God which are hidden from human knowledge and must, therefore, be revealed to those for whom they are intended."[1]

God calls human marriage "a great *musterion.*" *This is a great mystery: but I speak concerning Christ and the church* (Ephesians 5:32*).* The Greek word *megas,* translated "great," means:

great in external form or appearance;
great in size, weight, extent, measure, and stature;
great in quantity, age, and might;
great in importance, excellence, and value.

What is this huge, powerful, valuable thing of major importance to God? One part of this mystery is still to be revealed; the future marriage in heaven of Christ to The Church – The Bride of Christ (Revelation 21:2,16,17). The other part is the fact that you and your wife are one, a depiction of that future marriage. This part we can know and understand now.

Ephesians 5:31-32 *For this cause shall a man leave his father and mother, and shall be joined* (glued or welded facing each other) *unto his wife, and they two shall be one flesh. This is a great mystery: but I speak concerning Christ and the church.* (Note added by author.)

In Chapter Seven, I proposed that marriage is intended to be the reuniting of the creation of mankind – two becoming one again. God sums it up as:

Matthew19: 4-6a *And he answered and said unto them, Have ye not read, that he which made them at the beginning made them male and female, And said, For this cause shall a man leave father and mother, and shall cleave to his wife: and they twain shall be one flesh? Wherefore they are no more twain, but one flesh.*

CREATION	SEPARATION	MARRIAGE
step 1	**step 2**	**Step 3**
Two in one	One into two	Two into one

Figure 14.1 Elements of a Biblical Marriage

Notes On Ephesians 5:22-32

1. Wives in willing submission to their husbands (verse 22). (For the Biblical difference between obedience and submission, see Appendix C.)

2. Husbands are, and should act as, active heads over their wives (vs.23). Unlike Adam acted in the Garden, present but passive in his non-protection of the woman (Genesis 3:6). God made man to take dominion, first over himself, then his family, and finally over the physical universe. Passivity is a denial of what God created man to be.

3. As The Church is under submission to Christ, wives should submit to their husbands in the same manner (verse 24).

4. Husbands are commanded to love (*agape*) their wives in the same sacrificial way Christ loves The Church (verse 25).

5. Husbands are to sanctify their wives as Christ does The Church (verses 26 and 27). These verses indicate that Christ brings His Bride to salvation (separated and bathed); and keeps her pure (2 Corinthians11:2). (See also, John 13:10; Hebrews10:22; Revelation 1:5; cp. 1Corinthians 7:14,16). Like Christ, a man's word should provide his wife leadership with clear instructions in truth and love.

6. Husbands are obligated to love their wives with the same concern and devotion as Christ does The Church, nourishing and cherishing them (verses 28 and 29b). This could well include making it easy for them to submit.

Ephesians 5:33 *Nevertheless let every one of you in particular so love his wife even as himself; and the wife see that she reverence her husband.*

God's conclusion for His instructions on human marriage is to reveal the fact that the mystery of marriage in the garden was a part of His plan for mankind and for all of time. (The Church was not an after-thought in God's plan due to Israel's rejection of the Messiah.)

It is an awesome responsibility to represent Christ and The Church and thus testify before all mankind. Only through a right marriage union can mankind carry out God's mandates to rule the earth and its living creatures – be fruitful and multiply, and subdue all creation (Genesis 1:26,28). These are not one-man jobs; and they are definitely not one-woman jobs either.

How Has Men's Love for Women Been Damaged?

I previously stated that I believe Satan is actively trying to destroy men's love and women's submission (and thereby destroy marriage) through:

• Role reversal – caused by feminists movements and the emasculation of men;

• Lust – by romanticism for women and pornography for men;

• Perversion – homosexuality.

Ultimately the attack is against the separate roles of men and women. Satan attacks these by deceit – he first tempts the parties to be *dissatisfied* with their present positions, then to *doubt* God's word about their roles, and finally to *disobey* God's commands. Example:

• Satan tempted Eve to be *dissatisfied* with her restriction of fruit in the garden and her lack of knowledge:

Genesis 3:1 *Now the serpent was more subtle than any beast of the field which the LORD God had made. And he said unto the woman, Yea, hath God said, Ye shall not eat of every tree of the garden?* and,

Genesis 3:5 *For God doth know that in the day ye eat thereof, then your eyes shall be opened, and ye shall be as gods, knowing good and evil.*

• Then Satan tempted Eve to *doubt* God's warning of punishment;

Genesis 3:4 *And the serpent said unto the woman, Ye shall not surely die.*

• Thereby, Eve was *deceived* into unwittingly disobeying God;

Genesis 3:6 *And when the woman saw that the tree was good for food, and that it was pleasant to the eyes, and a tree to be desired to make one wise, she took of the fruit thereof, and did eat, and gave also unto her husband with her; and he did eat.*

• In this one act of *disobedience*, Eve abandoned her

role of helpmate to Adam and became instead his leader by inviting him to join her in sin.

• God's punishment (natural consequences for sin) for Eve was pain in child-bearing and worse, subordination in the marriage relationship:

Genesis 3:16 *Unto the woman he said, I will greatly multiply thy sorrow and thy conception; in sorrow thou shalt bring forth children;* **and thy desire shall be to thy husband, and he shall rule over thee**. (Emphasis is authors.)

Willful women have always been dissatisfied with their God-ordained position of subordination and have attempted to escape this curse for centuries. It is extremely difficult for a man to love a dissatisfied wife who wants to escape her role. The feminist movement has merely tapped into women's long-standing rebellion of heart and organized them. However, God always provides a grace blessing for those who adjust to any curse man earns. Certainly, women throughout history who have borne children; as well as those who have willingly submitted to their husbands' leadership, have been abundantly blessed through their acceptance of God's plan.

The counter thrust to Satan's attack has been the fifty-year emasculation of America's men discussed in previous chapters. These two factors engage in warfare in the stadium called 'marriage.'

• The average, emasculated husband must negotiate for his legitimate needs in marriage. This makes marriage like a partnership, with everything important being decided by vote or by trade-out. (Tragically, most Christian books on marriage today advise men not to exercise leadership over their wives. This false teaching supports the man's emasculation and the woman's rebellion at the same time.)

• The balance of today's married males are the effeminate types who avoid all conflict by simply allowing their wives to make all of the decisions and telling them what to do, just as Eve told Adam.

• Even the manliest of today's husbands have a difficult time leading their wives and families.

• Most of the macho types are either in, or in between, one of their divorces or affairs. They seldom have any real relationships and instead pursue their own gratification and entertainment.

Something for Everyone

If emasculated men and liberated women were not enough to destroy a man's love for a woman, marriage, and family; pornography and romanticism could finish the job. *These* (pornography and romanticism) *are just two faces of the same illusion – unattainable lust.* Romanticism started, "in the late 1700's as an artistic and intellectual movement in Europe. It emphasized nature, individual expression of emotion and imagination, and rebellion against established social roles and conventions."[2]

Another definition is, "impractical romantic ideas and attitudes, heroic times or adventures, lusty heroines and their rugged swains."[3] (Note: a swain is a lover.)

Romanticism became the diversion of many married women in 1800's America. They read poems, sonnets, and stories about impossible loves where the man was often a young, outdoor type and they were the heroines. These imaginary adventures allowed women to escape their less-exciting lives. Soap operas and Harlequin-type romantic novels today have taken the place of those superior literary counterparts of the 1800's. Whatever their intent, such sirens of emotion, imagination, and rebellion have served to call or encourage untold numbers of married women to dissatisfaction with their own husbands and comparatively mundane lives.

For the man's lusty appetite, Satan provided pornography. This illusion of forbidden sex has lured many a man to his destruction. Men do not want to read about relationships in romantic novels, they lust to see women – ankle, leg, or whatever. Pastors and other moral leaders have always taught against the existence of pornography. There must have been general agreement among men of the early 1800's, since every state outlawed pornography during the Victorian era (note that women could not vote then). The Supreme Court nullified these laws with their evil decisions in the 1950's. After that no one was allowed to define what was pornographic or obscene, therefore, no law could ban it. (Since the 1960's, violent sex crimes have increased five hundred percent, with eighty-six percent of rapists and eighty-seven percent of child molesters admitting to using pornography regularly to feed their fantasies. Pornography also feeds a man's macho attitudes of contempt for women, making his aggression toward real women more justifiable in his eyes.)

A man can become dissatisfied with his own wife's figure, sexual appetite, or general attitude toward sex when compared to the staged pictures and descriptions provided by pornography. With this tool, Satan has found a way to damage many men's love for their wives. Pornography insults the beauty of womanhood and instead portrays the woman as an instrument of unbridled sexual pleasure meant solely for the man's use and benefit. A man, therefore, can become dissatisfied with the wife of his youth and mother of his children. He can then disobey God's Word about fidelity. In self-deception he is likely to search for the illusion of endless enjoyment, which he imagines exists in 'free' sex. However, nothing is without cost:

Proverbs 5:3-5 *For the lips of a strange woman drop as an honeycomb, and her mouth is smoother than oil: But her end is bitter as wormwood, sharp as a two-edged sword. Her feet go down to death; her steps take hold on hell.* (He may be deluded enough to: *sin against his own body,* 1Corinthians 6:18.)

Finally, for those whose senses are too dulled with sin, over stimulation, drugs or alcohol, there is the lure of the rotten fruit of homosexuality, which if embraced, can harden their souls forever against God. I personally have heard of two, professing Christian husbands/fathers recently who left their families for males – unthinkable! What pain this must be for those wives and their children left behind; please pray for them.

Can JUDGMENT for the Church be far behind? (1 Peter 4:17) Who can doubt that the world-wide epidemic of sexually-transmitted diseases is the natural consequence of mankind's sins? Men, may I encourage you to keep yourselves pure; and to *cherish* (sacrificially love, nourish, provide for the needs and protection of) your wives as one of your top priorities in life!

Proverbs 5:18 *Let thy fountain be blessed: and rejoice with the wife of thy youth.*

Job 31:1 *I made a covenant with mine eyes; why then should I think upon a maid?*

Parenting and Family

Genesis 18:19a *For I know him, that he will command his children and his household after him, and they shall keep the way of the LORD, to do justice and judgment;.*

Proverbs 20:7 *The just man walketh in his integrity: his children [are] blessed after him*

1 Timothy 3:4,5 *One that ruleth well his own house, having his children in subjection with all gravity; (For if a man know not how to rule his own house, how shall he take care of the church of God?)*

Joshua 24:15b *but as for me and my house, we will serve the LORD.*

The chief responsibilities of a Christian man who is head of household are requiring order, leading, and teaching.

Requiring Order: He is commanded to bring up his children to be obedient and respectful (honoring) to both parents. This is an entire subject, which is covered thoroughly by my book, *What the Bible Says About... Child Training.*[4] I suggest that you and your wife study the verses quoted in that book and become experts on Biblical child training.

Leading: A man's entire family – wife, children, relatives and even domestics living with them – are required to follow his leadership: *but as for me and my house, we will serve the LORD* (Joshua 4:15b).

Teaching: God gives clear and repeated instructions for the man to be the one to teach his family about Him and His plan (Deuteronomy 6:4-7; Psalm 78:2-5). (The fact that men have abdicated this responsibility and that women have filled the void is a sign of our apostasy today.)

Government

Deuteronomy 1:13 *Take you wise men, and understanding, and known among your tribes, and I will make them rulers over you.*

Proverbs 8:16 *By me princes rule, and nobles, even all the judges of the earth.*

1Timothy 2:2 *For kings, and for all that are in authority; that we may lead a quiet and peaceable life in all godliness and honesty.*

Romans 13:1 *Let every soul be subject unto the higher powers. For there is no power but of God: the powers that be are ordained of God.*

Some politically conservative Christians believe God *may* be able to control other forms of government, but we Christians have to help control America because it is a republic. I hate to burst this bubble, but God can and does control our government like any other. He knew and allowed the overthrow of America's truly unique, constitutional 'republic' for its present form of mob-rule called 'democracy.' Actually, it could be shown that our present government (like all democracies) is really an oligarchy; 'rule by the few.' The masses are led to believe they have one-man-one-vote-rule, but 'the few' really are the ones who pull all of the strings.

God has also allowed us to subvert a mainly, Biblically-based legal system into a game of law instead of a system of justice. Our new system promotes immorality – abortion, divorce, homosexuality, pornography, anti-parental rights, law suits without substance, prisoners' rights, and has allowed wars unnecessary to defend our national boarders. Some of the major travesties in our law system have been: doing away with Biblically-defined accountability of any false-witnesses (which should include attorneys who bring false charges), plea bargaining, prison terms instead of requiring restitution, any appeals without legitimate proof, any consideration of supposed mental excuses, and of course, restriction of the death penalty.

Obviously, another entire book could be written about Biblical government and law (as well as one about church leadership), but we will have to save those for other projects. The next chapter will discuss Fatherhood as another extremely important role of men.

Notes

1. Greek, *musterion* "mystery." The unrevealed thoughts, plans, and historical timing of God, which are hidden from human knowledge and, therefore, must be revealed to those for whom they are intended. (Foundation for Biblical Research," Marriage.")

2. & 3. Romanticism; the emotional movement of the 1800's. Victorian literature flooded America (book sales increased *250%* from 1820

to 1860). *Womanhood in America*, by Mary P. Ryan. New York: Franklin Watts, 1983

4. *What the Bible Says About...Child Training*, J. Richard Fugate, 1980 Foundation for Biblical Research.

1Timothy 3:4 *One that ruleth well his own house, having his children in subjection with all gravity;*

1 Thessalonians 2:11 *As ye know how we exhorted and comforted and charged every one of you, as a father doth his children,*

CHAPTER FIFTEEN

BEING A FATHER

God's role for fatherhood has been the same throughout time. A man is to be the leader/authority over his family. He is to be head disciplinarian, teacher of character and spiritual truth to all his children, model of manhood for his sons, and model of a proper husband for his daughters. In the Old Testament, God referred to Abraham as the model patriarch (family head):

Genesis 18:19a *For I know him, that he will command his children and his household after him, and they shall keep the way of the LORD, to do justice and judgment;*

In the New Testament, God continued to use a similar description for a father who led and utilized authority properly over his children and household, thus qualifying him, like Abraham, to serve Him:

1 Timothy 3:4 *One that ruleth well his own house, having his children in subjection with all gravity*

The "one" in this passage is a man being considered for the function of an overseer in a local church (the position of elder). This man is said to lead his household by his consistent use of right standards (ones that are morally correct); and who always maintains control over his children due to their awesome respect (for his willingness to utilize his God-given authority). Notice that God does not make the woman responsible for leadership in the home or as primary ruler over the children. The Biblical man must function in this leadership position. Even the children sense that he should be in control and will tend to reject their mother's leadership (especially young men twelve years old and older) without his active participation.

Being a father utilizes all of the roles of Biblical manhood – leadership, provision, protection, and love. A modern-day patriarch does not habitually plop in front of the television, newspaper, or computer; nor does he involve himself in continuous reeducation, self-centered play, or long-term projects away from the family. However, I also know that most men need private time and a break from the stress of their demanding or boring jobs. I recommend you get up one hour earlier and spend private time speaking to God in prayer and allowing Him to speak to you while you read His Word. Then, exercise some, have breakfast, and plan your day. Another suggestion is to have your wife provide you some alone time every evening when you first arrive home from work. She could feed the children earlier (they will not mind), have them run around the house ten times, get them started on their baths, or anything in order to give you a break. This is an excellent time for you to discuss your work with your wife, making her more a part of your life that she longs to be. The only discussion that should not be allowed at this time is problems with the house, appliances, cars, finances, or children. There will be time and energy to deal with these *after* you change gears. If you need more personal activity time, try making your activity a family one. Fathers can teach their children while walking, biking, working around the house, or many other normal activities. Your children learn more from observing you in action than by just hearing your words. Christ states the importance of this:

John 5:19,20 *The Son can do nothing of himself, but what he seeth the Father do: for what things soever he doeth, these also doeth the Son likewise. For the Father loveth the Son, and sheweth him all things that himself doeth: and he will shew him greater works than these, that ye may marvel*

Lead by Example

Proverbs 20:7 *The just man walketh in his integrity: his children are blessed after him*

How we parents live our lives in front of our children will affect their view of God, ourselves, and themselves. If parents, especially the leader Dad, allows 'entertainment' to be seen by any of the family that promotes violence, drugs, and sex, he sets those things as acceptable standards. It is like a man who ogles every scantily clad girl he sees while in front of his young daughter. It should come as no surprise when she begins to dress, wear make-up, and even act like a Lolita in her pre-teens and older – desperately trying to get her Dad's attention. The wife who has to see this behavior in her husband becomes defeated and demoralized, thinking she can not compete with the bodies and young faces 'her man' so obviously desires. She becomes cold through this torture; and pleases him less than she could and would if she knew she were "his one and only." The son picks-up the father's obvious disrespect for womanhood. He is likely to develop a disdain for all women and a macho-type mentality that wants to use women only in a vain attempt to fulfill his lust. Better that men follow Scripture:

Job 31:1 *I made a covenant with mine eyes; why then should I think upon a maid?*

But, what if you are a 'religious' man who attends church, gives to the needy, and all that other stuff? (This man is not one with a personal relationship with Jesus Christ, but one who is dependent on his good deeds.) The hypocrisy that a religious man must live by is apparent to everyone except himself. His children often grow up either to hate him; or to continue his farce, as is mentioned in this verse:

2 Kings 17:41 *So these nations feared the LORD, and served their graven images, both their children, and their children's children: as did their fathers, so do they unto this day*

Obviously, it is easier for your children to accept evil than to imitate good, since their sin nature is naturally susceptible to evil. If we men live a double standard before our children (i.e. "Do what I say, not what I do."), the results will be woefully predictable. Whether we know it or not, our lives will have an impact on three or four generations:

Numbers 14:18 *The LORD is longsuffering, and of great mercy, forgiving iniquity and transgression, and by no means clearing the guilty, visiting the iniquity of the fathers upon the children unto the third and fourth generation*

But, it does not have to be a negative impact. You can also influence your children and their children positively; it is all up to you:

Proverbs 20:7 *The just man walketh in his integrity: his children are blessed after him*

One of the greatest things we men can pass on to our sons (besides salvation and a commitment to follow God's Word) is true masculinity and the willingness to stand for truth and righteousness. Hear the plea of King David from his deathbed to his son Solomon:

1 Kings 2:2 *I go the way of all the earth: be thou strong therefore, and shew thyself a man;*

God is still looking for champions in every generation who will stand for His righteousness and protect His people from the Enemy:

Ezekiel 22:30 *And I sought for a man among them, that should make up the hedge, and stand in the gap before me for the land, that I should not destroy it: but I found none.*

Isaiah 21:8b *My lord, I stand continually upon the watchtower in the daytime, and I am set in my ward whole nights.*

1 Corinthians 16:13 *Watch ye, stand fast in the faith, quit you like men, be strong.*

I am reminded of the 1858, Duffield Jr. hymn:

> *Stand up, stand up for Jesus, ye soldiers of the cross;*
> *Lift high His royal banner, it must not suffer loss.*

From victory unto victory His army shall He lead,
Till every foe is vanquished, and Christ is King indeed.

Even if you have not been a mature and godly man in your child's life thus far, could you make a solemn oath to God at this time: to train your sons to become soldiers of the cross from this point?

What Things Do I Teach?

Generally, you should never demean the natural characteristics of womanhood – instead, teach your son to have respect for all women (especially his mother). He will learn lessons for a lifetime when he sees you always taking the dirty jobs away from Mom; like servicing the car, picking up his dirty clothes, cleaning up after his projects, and watching out for her safety at all times.

You must not ridicule or express anger toward authority figures and he must not be allowed to either.

Teach him to be a gentleman at all times. You and his mother should teach him to have consideration for others through the practice of good manners. This means he is required to ... *in lowliness of mind let each esteem others better than themselves* (Philippians 2:3). Some of the behavior this covers are: not interrupting the conversations of others, especially adults; controlling loud talking and making loud noises in confined spaces (houses, restaurants, church buildings, etc.); controlling all crude body noises; observing the privacy of others; and respecting other people's private property.

He should be made to stand accountable for all of his responsibilities: cleanliness, schedules, duties, carelessness, deeds, and words. Teach your son to develop absolute trustworthiness in word and deed. He should learn to tell the truth even when it will cost him personally. And of course any stealing, cheating or lying is never to be tolerated.

The following verses are only a few of those given throughout Scripture about sons being instructed by their fathers.

Proverbs 4:1-4 *Hear, ye children, the instruction of a father, and attend to know understanding. For I give you good doctrine, forsake ye not my law. For I was my father's son, tender and only beloved in the sight of my mother. He taught me also, and said unto me, Let thine heart retain my words: keep my commandments, and live*

Hebrews 12:7 *If ye endure chastening, God dealeth with you as with sons; for what son is he whom the father chasteneth not?* (Corporal punishment.)

Obviously, a father has all of the authority he might need to bring his son's character and behavior into line with God's Word. But force, even when legitimate, is not the only way to influence and train your children. Your open expression of affection for your wife reinforces respect for womanhood and true love for your wife. Children are enchanted by seeing their parents' hug or kiss. They seem to gain a feeling of security by sharing your affections with them. Parents can also teach Christian service by example. Every time you volunteer to serve at church (deacon, committee, visitation, evangelism, or food to shut-ins) you demonstrate your willingness to serve others without personal gain. Your children should be required to assist you in these tasks until they can volunteer on their own. (If you have a child who has an inclination toward self-centeredness or feeling sorry for herself, I suggest she be required to serve others either with you or on her own until her attitude improves.) Make sure that your wife and children do not suffer because you are serving other families too much. Your family is the number one priority for your service. Be aware that your children are little 'spiritual fruit inspectors' always observing you to see if God works through you.

The Overwhelming Task of Fatherhood

If a man is not overwhelmed by this task, he just does not grasp the full scope of his responsibilities. No wonder the fathers of one hundred years ago abdicated their child rearing and family duties. It is far easier to work and receive instant feedback (pay) than it is to train your children day after day without knowing for sure what the results will be. This book is calling you back to your Biblical role. A father who truly understands what he may be getting himself into should be terrified; that is if he is limited to his own resources. However, proper fatherhood might be the test God has designed specifically for you to become totally dependant on Him. *For it is God which worketh in you both to will and to do of his good pleasure* (Philippians 2:13). Therefore, knowing your inadequacy may be a gift.

The sacrifice of fatherhood makes real heroes out of the common man. When a man dedicates himself to his wife and children, he commits himself to sacrifice careers, dreams, and opportunities. The hero may take a job that has excellent health benefits so his family will receive proper medical care. He will often enslave himself in a dead-end job that he hates; and then work there for twenty or thirty years to provide security for his family. Heroes will work two jobs if necessary. They willingly give up their dreams of having an interesting career, flying lessons, and that hunting/fishing trip to Alaska. Our country desperately needs Christian men who will live as heroes for God.

SECTION FOUR CONCLUSION

Congratulations! You have just completed a rather difficult book containing information and challenges new to you. *Nobody* ever said that "Being a Man" would be easy. But, by completing this book you have already displayed self-discipline, commitment, and a desire to follow God. I trust you have also grown in understanding about your Biblical roles and confidence in how to live them. I especially pray that you have grown in *agape* love toward your wife, your children, and your neighbors. The Christian knows that even if he has all knowledge but has not *agape*, he is nothing (from 1 Corinthians 13:2).

I trust you have gained a greater appreciation and understanding for your helpmate through these writings. You should be more than willing to protect her due to her delicacy (vulnerability). You also should appreciate her loyalty in standing beside you on your hapless journey through the unknown. Do not be discouraged if you find yourself much like a child due to lack of training and/or knowledge of God's teaching. Instead, commit yourself now to becoming a man:

1Corinthians13:11 *When I was a child, I spake as a child, I understood as a child, I thought as a child: but when I became a man, I put away childish things.*

Developing character and exercising leadership will be the most difficult projects for most modern men. You could do it by yourself with God's power. However, I have a couple suggestions that could make your new journey easier and faster:

• Give a copy of this book to your pastor and request his evaluation concerning the church having a special men's class based on the material covered. He could teach or assign the job to a mature man in the congregation. A student workbook will be ready in 2003 or the teacher can put together his own teacher's guide. (Please e-mail me the results of your class, cbg@rfugate.org.)

• Meet with one or more men who have read the book themselves and want to join with a discussion group. Some men will want to pick accountability partners out of this group.

• At least reread this book and make yourself a complete set of notes. Measure your personal progress on a chart.

The material benefits from your becoming a Biblically mature man are the natural fruits you will enjoy. (Mature men usually make a better living and are often promoted to leadership positions.) The soul fruit will be the improved character you will develop. The Spiritual gain will be in living your life to the glory of God.

May God bless you on your renewed journey through this life. You have now answered the challenge to be one of the "few good men" in God's army.

To God be the glory,

J. Richard Fugate

APPENDIX A

THE BIBLE AS A SOURCE OF INFORMATION FOR MAN

The following development sets forth why the author looks to the Bible for the truth man should live by, and this discussion establishes the Bible as the basic premise for this book.

God Exists:

> *In the beginning God created the heaven and the earth* (Genesis 1:1).

> *Before the mountains were brought forth, or ever thou hast formed the earth and the world, even from everlasting to everlasting, thou art God* (Psalm 90:2).

The Bible never attempts to prove or explain God's existence. It simply declares it to be true. This book, therefore, begins with this absolute: God's existence is certain truth. The Bible further states that no man can escape the recognition of the fact that God does exist:

> *Because that which may be known of God is manifest in them; for God hath shown it unto them. For the invisible things of him from the creation of the world are clearly seen, being understood by the things that are made, even his eternal power and Godhead; so that they are without excuse:* (Romans 1:19 & 20).

Man may attempt to reject God, but man can never honestly deny his knowledge of God's existence. This passage reveals that God has made Himself known to man both rationally and empirically. The knowledge of the existence of God has been placed by God within the rational perception of man's mind. Creation, through its order and consistency, clearly presents the empirical proof of God the Creator. Acceptance of the knowledge of the existence of God as Creator will lead to the next logical assumption.

Mankind Exists as a Creation of God:

> *So God created man in his own image, in the image of God created he him; male and female created he them* (Genesis 1:27).

Man as a creature is dependent on his Creator, God. As Creator, God is responsible for His creation. To bring a creature into existence, but to fail to provide for the needs of that creature would be an act of irresponsibility. Because God cares for His creatures and takes full responsibility for His creation, He has provided for man's needs.

God Has Provided for Mankind's Physical Needs:

> *And God blessed them, and God said unto them, be fruitful, and multiply, and fill the earth, and subdue it; and have dominion over the fish of the sea, and over the fowl of the air, and over every living thing that moveth upon the earth. And God said, Behold, I have given you every herb bearing seed, which is upon the face of all the earth, and every tree, in which is the fruit of a tree yielding seed; to you it shall be for food* (Genesis 1:28, 29).

The Hebrew word translated "to subdue" means "to tread down with the feet, to dominate";[1] and the word translated "dominion" means "to rule."[2] Man was given the command to rule all earth's living creatures. He was given the command to control and use all earth's resources. God's provision for man's physical needs is the entire physical universe including air, water, land, plants, living creatures, and the climatic range required for man's existence. Physical science recognizes the extremely narrow range of environment in which man can survive and how perfectly it has been arranged to support all man's physical requirements.

Man is not merely a physical creation that exists in only a physical universe. He is also a creation of soul and spirit. As such, he has needs of the soul and the spirit, not just physical needs. In taking full responsibility for His creation, God has also provided for all man's soul and spiritual needs just as completely as He has for the physical.

God Has Provided for Mankind's Soul and Spiritual Needs:

> *But he answered and said, It is written, Man shall not live by bread alone, but by every word that proceedeth out of the mouth of God* (Matthew 4:4).

Bread is the example of God's physical provision, while God's Word is God's provision for man's soul and spiritual life. God's Word has been provided for man's benefit. It has been recorded and preserved according to the faithfulness and justice of God. Because God cares for His creation, He has provided all that man needs to live;

not only to survive physically, but to live abundantly in both soul and spirit.

Man was given the ability by God to subdue the physical universe and to rule the living things. Man was given strength and dexterity, but above all he was given mentality. With this mentality man could, on his own, discover the principles by which God governs the physical universe. Man has gradually obtained knowledge of the physical universe by observation of these natural laws, in other words, by science. Geology, astronomy, physiology, and mathematics are examples of true science. By contrast, the principles that govern the soul and spirit of man are not of a physical nature and cannot be discovered through the mentality of man.

Man has the need to understand his own soul, to know how to relate to other human beings, and to know his proper relationship with the physical universe. When man attempts to discover soul information by means of his own mentality apart from God's revelation, he is limited to his ability to observe and to reason. He therefore invents the pseudo-sciences of psychology, sociology, and anthropology in an attempt to answer man's soul questions and to solve man's soul problems.

Man also has the need to understand his spiritual relationship to His Creator, God. He needs to know where he came from, where he is going, who he is, and why he exists. Without knowing his own origin, destiny, make-up, and purpose, man is disoriented to life – even though he is physically alive. When man attempts to discover spiritual information by means of his own intellect apart from God's revelation, he develops various types of pseudo knowledge such as philosophy and religion, both of which are man-centered.

For soul and spiritual knowledge, man is totally dependent on God. Man cannot discover the principles that govern the soul or the spirit apart from the information that God has provided. God's Word is infinitely superior to any thought man could possibly have.

God's Thinking is Superior to Man's:

For my thoughts are not your thoughts, neither are your ways my ways, saith the Lord. For as the heavens are higher than the earth, so are my ways higher than your ways, and my thoughts than your thoughts (Isaiah 55:8,9).

God's thinking is far beyond the ability of man. It is foolish for man in his arrogance to question God's Word by means of his own viewpoint. As God declares:

He that trusteth in his own heart is a fool, (Proverbs 28:26a).

When God presents information on any subject, it will naturally conflict with the human systems of thinking. Human philosophy, psychology, sociology, or religion apart from God's Word is the attempt of mere man to organize thoughts that are inferior to God's thoughts. These systems of thinking must be evaluated by God's Word, not God's Word by them.

Each person's opinions are a combination of these human systems of thinking plus their own experiences. As the

Biblical position is presented, it will be necessary for the reader to evaluate objectively his existing opinion by God's Word.

The Bible is God's Word

The Bible declares itself to be God's Word:

> *All scripture is given by inspiration of God, and is profitable for doctrine, for reproof, for correction, for instruction in righteousness,* (2 Timothy 3:16).

> *Knowing this first, that no prophecy of the scripture is of any private interpretation. For the prophecy came not at any time by the will of man, but holy men of God spoke as they were moved by the Holy Spirit* (2 Peter 1:20, 21).

God did not cause His Word to be recorded for His own benefit, but to benefit mankind. It is a complete instruction manual containing soul and spiritual principles; therefore, mankind can look to the Bible for the information he needs on any moral or spiritual issue. The Bible has the answer for all of man's non-physical questions from eternal salvation to every practical matter in life. It is the only true source of moral and spiritual information by which man can successfully live each day. Since God's Word is to benefit man, it is meant to be understood.

Mankind is Meant to Understand God's Word:

> *The secret things belong unto the Lord our God; but those things which are revealed belong unto*

us and to our children forever, that we may do all
the words of this law (Deuteronomy 29:29).

God is infinite and omniscient. He has not revealed all
His knowledge to finite man, but what He has revealed
can both be understood and utilized. God's information
is available to those who diligently search out its meaning
and can be used successfully by those who accept its
teaching. God has not hidden His soul and spiritual
provision from mankind. God's Word is dependable and
verifiably true.

God's Word Equals Truth:

thy word is truth (John 17:17b).

It is impossible for God to lie (Hebrews 6:18). The Bible
presents true principles (or laws) which can be applied in
practice with predictable results. There are natural, fixed
consequences for either observing or violating the soul
and spiritual laws just as surely as for violating the physical
laws. No man would expect to violate the law of gravity
and not pay the consequences, but he will often foolishly
violate soul and spiritual principles with total abandon.
When physical laws are properly observed, the results
are predictable and beneficial to man. Proper observance
of the soul and spiritual principles will also produce
consistent, beneficial results. God's Word declares the
natural consequences of either observing or violating truth.

Observing Truth Results in Blessing
Violating Truth Results in Cursing

And it shall come to pass, if thou shalt hearken
diligently unto the voice of the Lord thy God, to

observe and to do all his commandments which I command thee this day, that the Lord thy God will set thee on high above all nations of the earth; And all these blessings shall come on thee, and overtake thee, if thou shalt hearken unto the voice of the Lord thy God (Deuteronomy 28:1, 2).

But it shall come to pass, if thou wilt not hearken unto the voice of the Lord thy God, to observe to do all his commandments and his statutes which I command thee this day, that all these curses shall come upon thee, and overtake thee (Deuteronomy 28:15).

I have set before you life and death, blessing and cursing; therefore, choose life, that both thou and thy seed may live, Joshua 1:8 This book of the law shall not depart out of thy mouth, but thou shalt meditate therein day and night, that thou mayest observe to do according to all that is written therein; for hen thou shalt make thy way prosperous, and then thou shalt have good success (Deuteronomy 30:19b).

Notes

1 Hebrew, *kabash* "subdue, bring into bondage, tread down with the feet;" thus "to dominate" (Zechariah 9:15; Micah 7:19; Jeremiah 34:11, 16; 2 Chronicles 28:10; Nehemiah 5:5). In Genesis 1:28 the aspect of "control" is evident and *kabash* is in the imperative mood of command. (Foundation for Biblical Research)

2 Hebrew, *radah* "have dominion, rule, dominate" over someone or something; used here to indicate a position of dominance once the subduing has been accomplished. Like *kabash, radah* is a command. God commands man to "subdue" and then "rule" over that which has been subdued. (Ibid.)

APPENDIX B

CREATION OF THE SPECIES, MANKIND

Male and female, created as one, become one again through marriage.

...male and female created He them (Genesis 1:27)	...made He a woman and brought her unto the man (Genesis 2:22)	and they two shall be one flesh. (Ephesians 5:31b)
Step One ⎯⎯⎯⎯→	**Step Two** ⎯⎯⎯⎯→	**Step Three**
ADAM (mankind)	Ish and Ishshah	Marriage
Created as one	Two from one	One from two

Figure B.1

Male and female created he them; and blessed them, and called their name Adam, in the day when they were created (Genesis 5:2).

Both Genesis 1:27 and 5:2 use a very interesting choice of words translated "male" and "female" from the Hebrew language. They are *zakar* and *neqebah* which always refer to genders (maleness and femaleness), not specifically to a man and a woman. Sometimes these words refer to humans, like in these verses; but other times to animals, as in loading the ark two by two in Genesis 7:9.

There have been various opinions about the created order of mankind. For instance, does Genesis 1:27 give a general account of man's creation and then Genesis 2:7 add the details in Hebrewistic style, or is there an actual chronology of events being given? Obviously, since God later fashioned the woman from the materials out of the man He had previously manufactured, we know that at least man's body existed prior in time to her body. Also, we know that God breathed the breath of life directly into the man after his body was formed. So, there was at least some order in man's creation. Allow me to suggest a chronology, which I believe is true to the Biblical account and the plan of God. (A list of the nine Hebrew words God uses together only in these nine verses to describe creation is given below.):

> *And God said, Let us make man in our image, after our likeness* (Genesis 1:26a).

This verse views God planning the creation of mankind sometime *prior* to the sixth day.

> *In the day that God created man, in the likeness of God made he him:* (Genesis 5:1b).

This verse views mankind *after* its creation and as the first in man's genealogy. The Hebrew word used in both of these verses for "make" and "made" man is *asah*. This is the general word for the making or manufacturing of something out of raw materials.)

> *So God created man in his own image, in the image of God created he him; male and female created he them* (Genesis 1:27).

God creates (*bara*) the immaterial essence of both a male and a female human being out of nothing.

> *And the LORD God formed man of the dust of the ground, and breathed into his nostrils the breath of life; and man became a living soul* (Genesis 2:7).

God then forms (*yatsar* – the Hebrew word for molding or shaping something specific) the man's body out of the dust of the earth.

Here we have the formation and animation of a physical male body. The immaterial essence of both the male and the female God had already created may have been the lives breathed into this body to animate it. *The first man Adam was made a living soul;* (1Corinthians15:45a) The Greek word used here for "was made" means," to become something it was not before" – like to be born.

> *And the LORD God caused a deep sleep to fall upon Adam and he slept: and he took one of his ribs, and closed up the flesh instead thereof; And the rib, which the LORD God had taken from man, made he a woman, and brought her unto the man* (Genesis 2:21, 22).

Here we have the building of the woman's physical body. The Hebrew word translated "made" (*banah*) means to fashion or shape from existing materials.

The following listing of words helps point out the uniqueness of God's Word. The Bible uses four, distinctly different Hebrew words for His creative acts of mankind and five different words for naming His creation of The Man and The Woman. These nine words appear multiple times within only nine verses of Genesis. Nowhere else in Scripture do all of these words appear together:

> *asah* – to do, make, execute, work. This word in the creation account depicts the general activity of God in bringing about all of creation.

bara – to create something out of nothing; to bring into existence.

yatsar – to form or fashion a material substance like a potter.

banah – to build (up) a material into a structure.

AND;

adam – generic for mankind as a species; proper name for the first man.

zakar and *neqebah* – male and female gender of any species. (The Greek equivalence for these Hebrew words for gender are, *thelus* and *arsen*, and they are used together in Matthew 19:4; Mark 10:6; and Galatians 3:28.

ish and *ishshah* – man and woman as distinct entities (Genesis 2:23).

SUMMARY

Several factors should be emphasized at this point:

1. It is not said that the Woman had been animated by God's breath.

2. Scripture says, *woman was made of* (out of) *the man* (1Corinthians 11:8); *for* (because of) *the man* (not man because of the woman); and, *Adam was first* (in order) *formed, then Eve* (1Timothy 2:13).

3. We do know that the material used for the woman's *physical* body came directly from the man's body.

4. Is it not reasonable to surmise that her immaterial essence (or soul?) also came from The Man?

5. Consider this: Only after the female was completed was she called "Woman" (*ishshah*), meaning "out of Man;" and he was called "Man" (*ish*) for the first time, as they *then* became unique creations.

> *And Adam said, This is now bone of my bones, and flesh of my flesh: she shall be called Woman, because she was taken out of Man* (Genesis 2:23).

I believe God is speaking about more than flesh and bones in this and the next verse (Genesis 2:24). Marriage is the intertwining of the souls of a man and a woman, not merely their physical union. Certainly the prohibition in Matthew 19:6, *... let not man put asunder...* refers to the separation of man and woman beyond just their bodies. Therefore, Adam must have been identifying his soul-mate in Genesis 2:23 as well as his physical counterpart. Those of us who have this kind of relationship, as my wife and I have had for over forty-four years say, amen; and praise the God of all creation!

The following chart lays out in a chronological order all of the verses God used to describe the original creation of man and woman.

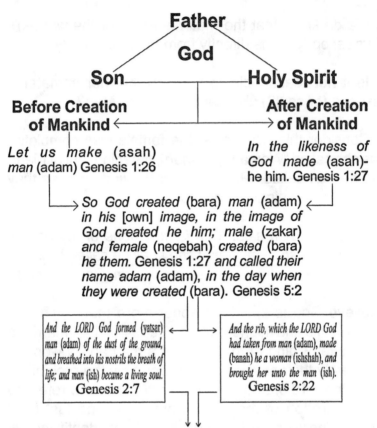

Father

God

Son ——————————————— **Holy Spirit**

Before Creation ←——————————→ **After Creation**
of Mankind   **of Mankind**

Let us make (asah)   *In the likeness of*
man (adam) Genesis 1:26   *God made* (asah)-
                               he him. Genesis 1:27

→ *So God created* (bara) *man* (adam) ←
in his [own] *image, in the image of*
God created he him; male (zakar)
and female (neqebah) *created* (bara)
he them. Genesis 1:27 *and called their*
name adam (adam), *in the day when*
they were created (bara). Genesis 5:2

| *And the LORD God formed* (yatsar) *man* (adam) *of the dust of the ground, and breathed into his nostrils the breath of life; and man* (ish) *became a living soul.* Genesis 2:7 | *And the rib, which the LORD God had taken from man* (adam), *made* (banah) *he a woman* (ishshah), *and brought her unto the man* (ish). Genesis 2:22 |

And Adam said, This is now bone of my bones,
and flesh of my flesh: Genesis 2:23a

and they shall be one flesh. Genesis 2:24b

and shall be joined unto his wife, and
they two shall be one flesh. Ephesians 5:31b

Wherefore they are no more twain, but one
flesh. What therefore God hath joined
together, let not man put asunder.
Matthew 19:6

Figure B.2 Chronology of Mankind's Creation

APPENDIX C

BIBLICAL DIFFERENCES BETWEEN OBEDIENCE AND SUBMISSION

Biblical submission is *not* synonymous with blind obedience! In order to understand the critical difference between submission and obedience, we need to discover the Biblical definition of each word.

Obedience

God's Word uses two distinctive Greek words, one for obedience and the other for submission, when referring to the function of various subordinates under proper authorities. The Greek word *hupakouo* is normally used in Scripture for obedience. Its technical meaning is "under the hearing of commands." A Biblical command for obedience is often followed by a promise of blessing to the subject who complies, or with a warning of negative consequences to the subject who chooses noncompliance. Under the command for obedience, the subordinate is offered no alternative but to obey, nor is he allowed to debate the question of whether he should or should not obey. The appointed authority enforces compliance, executes judgment, and stands responsible for the results of his rule. The only responsibility of the subject under obedience is to do what he is told.[1]

An example of the concept of obedience (as opposed to submission) is found in Colossians 3:22-25. Christian slaves were instructed to remain obedient to their masters and to serve wholeheartedly, as if they were serving the Lord Himself. The following verses give us two more examples of God's use of the word "obedience." In the first passage God commands children to obey their parents:

> *Children, obey your parents in the Lord; for this is right. Honor thy father and mother (which is the first commandment with a promise;) That it maybe well with thee, and thou mayest live long on the earth* (Ephesians 6:1-3).

The second passage concerns the importance of obedience to God:

> *And to you who are troubled, rest with us, when the Lord Jesus shall be revealed from heaven with his mighty angels, In flaming fire taking vengeance on them that know not God, and that **obey not** the gospel of our Lord Jesus Christ: Who shall be punished with everlasting destruction from the presence of the Lord, and from the glory of His power* (2 Thessalonians 1:7-9). (Emphasis added)

Obedience to the gospel of Jesus Christ refers to the personal acceptance of Christ as the only way to eternal salvation. This example warns that the consequences for disobedience (that is, non-acceptance of Christ as Savior) will be everlasting separation from the presence and power of the Lord.

Submission

The second Greek word used in the Bible when referring to the function of subordinates is *hupotasso,* which means submission. Technically, submission means "under placement or position of; status or rank." This word is used by the writers of Scripture to refer to the positions and attitudes of subjects under the authority of their government (I Peter 2:13-15), to believers under the teaching authority of their pastors (Hebrews 13:17), and of wives under the leadership of their husbands (Ephesians 5:22). The Biblical definition of submission includes the willing and positive response of a subordinate to his rightful authority. The submissive subject *consciously and freely yields* his or her own will to the will of the authority. [2]

An example of Biblical submission is Christ's submission to God the Father in the Garden of Gethsemane just prior to His death on the cross. Christ's example reveals that submission is not an act of blind obedience, but instead, is a conscious act of a subordinate choosing to yield his will to the will of his authority.

> *And he was withdrawn from them about a stone's cast, and kneeled down, and prayed, Saying, Father, if thou be willing, remove this cup from me: nevertheless, not my will, but thine, be done* (Luke 22:41-42).

Submission Versus Obedience

When God commands a subject to be obedient, the will of that subject is not considered and his only choice is compliance. For example, a child is to obey unquestionably the authority of his parents, and parents are instructed to enforce compliance, even against the child's will when necessary. However, when God commands a wife to submit to her husband's authority, He is requiring more of her than mere compliance. He is calling her to choose to submit in a Christ-like manner.

The Subordinate's Accountability to God

Another major difference between submission and obedience can be found in the level of responsibility that God places on a subordinate for his or her own actions and attitudes. In Acts 5:29; we are told that obedience to God takes precedence, whenever there is a conflict between God's command and man's decree. A Biblically submissive person is *willing* to comply, but, realizing that he/she still remains accountable to God for personal sin, they may choose to disobey *if* their authorities' request or command is a known violation of one of God's direct commands. If noncompliance is necessary, however, the Biblically submissive person continues to maintain the proper attitude of respect for their authorities' leadership position and for his overall right to lead. This action might be called, 'submissive noncompliance.'

Submissive Noncompliance

One Biblical example of submissive noncompliance is found in the sixth chapter of Daniel. In this passage the king enacted a law that *whosoever shall ask a petition of any God or man for thirty days save of thee, 0 king, he shall be cast into the den of lions* (Daniel 6:7b).

Obedience to the king's decree would have caused Daniel to sin against a direct command of God: *Thou shalt have no other gods before me* (Exodus 20:3). Therefore, it was necessary for Daniel to disobey the king's law. However, was his disobedience an act of self-righteous rebellion, or was it submissive noncompliance? It is imperative that we examine Daniel's attitude toward his king for the answer to this question.

In the first place, Daniel maintained a close personal relationship with God, even though it meant that he had to disobey his king.

> *Now when Daniel knew that the writing was signed, he went into his house; and his windows being open in his chamber toward Jerusalem, he kneeled upon his knees three times a day, and prayed, and gave thanks before his God, as he did aforetime* (Daniel 6:10).

Secondly, there is no indication that Daniel had a rebellious or defensive attitude toward his subordinate role as a subject under a king. He previously submitted to the king's authority in all things, and he did not disobey until the king passed a new law that directly opposed God's expressed will: that believers worship Him alone, praying and giving thanks. Although Daniel knew the dire consequences of choosing to disobey in this instance, he did not do so defiantly, nor did he run away from those consequences. Daniel continued to recognize the king's right to execute punishment as the duly appointed authority.

> *Then the king commanded, and they brought Daniel, and cast him into the den of lions* (Daniel 6:16a).

Thirdly, Daniel remained respectful of his king's position of authority. He was free from any rebellious or self-righteous attitudes before, during, and after his disobedience. Daniel's speech after God delivered him from the lions is a perfect example of willing submission to an authority in a situation requiring submissive noncompliance.

> *Then said Daniel unto the king, O king, live forever. My God hath sent His angel, and hath shut the lions' mouths, that they have not hurt me: forasmuch as before Him innocence was found in me; and also before thee, O king, have I done no hurt* (Daniel 6:21 – 22).

Keep in mind that Daniel said, "*O King live forever,*" to an authority that had just ordered his death.

Application to Wives

Daniel's example of submission is a far cry from the defiant "I'll never let a man tell me what to do," that we hear many women say today. Such outcries usually come from women who try to justify their refusal to obey God's command to submit to their husbands by claiming that he *might* ask them to do something that would violate their personal rights. Such women lie in wait, expecting their husbands to err, so that their before-the-fact attitude of non-submission will be vindicated. They often fabricate 'what if's' and treat the rare misuses of their husbands' authority as if they were common, everyday events. (I believe, the percentage of husbands who actually ask their godly wives to sin is very, very small. Therefore, for most women this is a moot point, born more from a desire to escape submission entirely, than a true concern over wronging

God.) The attitude of women who attempt to pre-justify non-submission is a continuation of the garden-variety rebelliousness that has existed since the fall of mankind. By contrast, Daniel's example is a testimony of what is possible when a believer obeys God by properly submitting to human authorities who actually do act unrighteously. Defiant subordinates in other authority structures often act in a similar manner.

No, obedience and submission are not synonymous. The difference, however, is not necessarily seen in one's overt actions. Obedience is an external act of compliance, while submission toward any authority is the respectful attitude that comes before, during, and after all actions. Where a list of rules and commands must precede obedience, submission precedes rules and supersedes law. Submission includes freedom of choice - the choice to obey God by freely yielding oneself to the authority He has placed over him/her. It involves trust -his or her absolute trust in the integrity of the God who designed the subordinates' role and included submission to authority within His plan. Submission is the natural result of a believers abiding trust in God, and it is the fruit of their desire to do His Will.

Notes

[1] Greek, *hupakouo* "obey." Compound word consisting of the preposition *hupo* "under" and *akouo* "hear;" literally "to hear under," thus to obey what is heard (Ephesians 6:1,5; Colossians 3:20,22; 2Thessalonians 1:8; 3:14). (Foundation for Biblical Research, "Child Training.").

[2] Greek, *hupotasso* "submit, subordinate." Compound word consisting of the preposition *hupo* "under" and *tasso* "put in place, station;"

literally "to place under," thus to submit to a position of authority (Romans 13:1,5; Ephesians 5:22,24; Titus 2:9,3:1; James 4:7; 1 Peter 2:13),

Conclusion: The distinction between *hupakouo* and *hupotasso* is that *hupakouo* emphasizes the strict following of verbal commands (mandatory compliance in action) regardless of personal willingness, while *hupotasso* emphasizes the attitude of voluntary compliance to the known will or position of another.

You may order additional copies of this book, *What the Bible Says About ... Being a Man*, (ISBN 1-889700-29-0) ($11.95) as well as the Fugate's other titles by writing or calling:

Family Ministries
PO Box 1412
Fair Oaks, CA 95628
Order Line: 1-800-545-1729

Inquires for quantity discounts are welcomed at:
cbg@rfugate.org
or call 916/729-6993

What the Bible Says About . . . Child Training
by J. Richard Fugate
ISBN 1-889700-13-4
($12.95)

This book is considered by many to be the deepest and most comprehensive work on Biblical child training ever written. It has the depth of a seminary textbook, yet the simplicity of a practical how-to manual. It is no wonder that *What the Bible Says About ... Child Training* has been accepted by thousands of Bible-believing churches as the standard text on child training for almost twenty years. This 2nd edition publication contains 80 new pages of author comments, examples, and anecdotes.

The unique aspect of *What the Bible Says About ... Child Training* is that the author accepts the Bible as absolute truth and infinitely superior to any human system of thinking. The system of child training presented has been used by over 250,000 families with dramatic results, thus providing the proof that testifies of all truth – IT WORKS!

What the Bible Says About . . . Suffering
by J. Richard Fugate
ISBN 1-889700-35-5
$12.00

Christians are not exempt from suffering in this life. Have you lost
a loved one, or had a severe physical ailment, or existed in a
struggling marriage." This book contains vital information for
spiritual growth and understanding regardless of how serious are
your struggles. *What the Bible Says About ... Suffering* answers
the question you may have asked, "Why does God allow His
people to suffer?" Fugate uses the Bible to reveal how God will
help you triumph over suffering and be victorious in your life!

"Why Suffering?" J. Richard Fugate bases his
discussion upon what the Bible says. He proffers
a systematic theology on suffering to replace
psychological programs found in modern
counseling. The first section addresses both the
Christian and non-Christian. It includes a well
thought out explanation to the question: Why
does mankind suffer? His analysis is Biblical,
theologically sound, and logical. I highly
recommend this book to begin a study of suffering
from God's point of view."

Dr. John C. Beck, Jr., Professor of
Theology
Chafer Theological Seminary
Orange, CA

On the Other Side of the Garden
Biblical Womanhood in Today's World
by Virginia Fugate
ISBN 0-86717-008-5
$10.00

The Biblical principles in this book have successfully been studied
and applied by thousands of women for over nine years. Subjects
covered are:

- Finding renewed purpose for your life.
- Distinguishing submission from blind obedience.
- Correctly influencing your husband, children, and church.
- Communicating your needs in a language men
  understand.
- Dealing with a passive, overbearing, or unspiritual man.
- Coping with disillusions, disappointments, and irritations in
  marriage.

(A study guide/workbook is also available for this book. $12.00)

Victorious Women *On the Other Side of the Garden*
by Virginia Ruth Fugate
ISBN 1-889700-25-8
$10.95

Where *On the Other Side of the Garden* presents the principles,
Victorious Women presents real life examples of Biblical
womanhood in action. Virginia comes alongside women in this
heartwarming sequel to her first book. She invites you to join her
on a journey through a garden of other women's victories as she
shares insights into Biblical womanhood. Her friendly format
provides an easy atmosphere in which the victories of real women
will encourage you to overcome the challenges of being a woman
in today's world. *On the Other Side of the Garden* was mind
changing; ***Victorious Women*** will encourage your heart!
